Series / Number 07-006

CANONICAL ANALYSIS
AND
FACTOR COMPARISON

MARK S. LEVINE
Research Department
Leo Burnett U.S.A.

SAGE PUBLICATIONS / Beverly Hills / London

For information address:

SAGE Publications, Inc.
275 South Beverly Drive
Beverly Hills, California 90212

SAGE Publications Ltd
28 Banner Street
London EC1Y 8QE

International Standard Book Number 0-8039-0655-2

Library of Congress Catalog Card No. L.C. 77-75941

THIRTEENTH PRINTING, 1988

When citing a professional paper, please use the proper form. Remember to cite the correct Sage University Paper series title and include the paper number. One of the two following formats can be adapted (depending on the style manual used):

(1) IVERSEN, GUDMUND R. and NORPOTH, HELMUT (1976) "Analysis of Variance." Sage University Paper series on Quantitative Applications in the Social Sciences, 07-001. Beverly Hills and London: Sage Pubns.

OR

(2) Iversen, Gudmund R. and Norpoth, Helmut. 1976. *Analysis of Variance.* Sage University Paper series on Quantitative Applications in the Social Sciences, series no. 07-001. Beverly Hills and London: Sage Publications.

CONTENTS

Editor's Introduction

CANONICAL ANALYSIS AND FACTOR COMPARISON are related techniques that allow a researcher to examine patterns of interrelationships *between sets of variables*. In most data analysis in the social sciences, the researcher is trying to predict the value of a dependent variable on the basis of a set of independent variables. Regression analysis permits the researcher to consider only *one* independent variable at a time. But with a background in regression analysis,* the researcher can progress to an understanding of more complex analysis.

CANONICAL ANALYSIS AND FACTOR COMPARISON extend the basic relationships to an entire set of dependent variables. The critical advantage that these techniques offer over simple regression analysis is, therefore, that they allow an examination of a wide variety of possible interrelationships. For example, this paper examines the relationship between expenditures across several policy areas and various social and political characteristics of nations. It examines the possible interrelationships among independent (social and political traits) variables and dependent variables (expenditure levels).

Both factor comparison and canonical analysis depend on identical mathematical skills—and both depend on an understanding of factor analysis.** Some of the mathematics in this advanced paper may lie outside the training of the reader; however, as the author notes, these sections may be skimmed for a general understanding without precise comprehension of the mathematical details.

In a series devoted to making methodology readily accessible to students and teachers with a limited knowledge of statistics and mathematics, why devote an issue to such a complex, advanced, and sophisticated technique?

The answer lies in the many and unique *applications* of CANONICAL ANALYSIS AND FACTOR COMPARISON:

- Political scientists might employ canonical correlation to determine— as demonstrated in this paper—which social and political attributes of

---

*For an introduction to the techniques of regression analysis, readers may consult two papers within this series: Eric Uslaner (forthcoming) *Regression Analysis: Simultaneous Equation Estimation* and Charles Ostrom (forthcoming) *Times Series Analysis*, both in the Sage University Papers on Quantitative Applications in the Social Sciences. Beverly Hills and London: Sage Publications.

**For an explanation of this subject see the paper in this series by Jae-On Kim (forthcoming) *Factor Analysis*. Sage University Paper on Quantitative Applications in the Social Sciences. Beverly Hills and London: Sage Publications.

nations have the greatest impact on expenditures across several policy areas.

• Sociologists might use canonical correlation to determine which factor—urbanization or income level—has the greater effect on the status awarded to a particular group of people, or which has the greatest effect on the crime rate of that group. Canonical correlation allows the researcher to determine not only whether each of the independent variables has an effect on the other dependent variables, but it will also help him establish which independent variable has the stronger relationship with each dependent variable.

• Psychologists might find factor comparison particularly useful. They might ask two groups of individuals to make judgements on a set of stimuli (such as a Rorschach Inkblots test or a tape-recording of electronic music). For each group tested, they could factor analyze the judgement ratings to assess the underlying dimensional configuration. They would then be able to make comparisons of the structure of the subjects' judgements, or make inferences about the subgroup similarities and differences between one set of raters and the other.

• Economists might use canonical correlation to study which educational and environmental attributes of groups have the greatest impact on their expenditures for housing, transportation, and the education of children.

• Education researchers might use factor comparison to contrast the learning curves of different groups of children to study which variables have the most direct effect on enhanced learning capability for different cultural subgroups.

• Social scientists of all disciplines need factor comparison to evaluate results when they have two factor analytic solutions to the same problem. Suppose that two different researchers employed the same data but used different techniques to analyze the facts—and announced divergent results! How different are their results? The researchers can make a determination and an overall measure of how different their configurations really are, by using factor comparison. Or consider a specific example: one researcher uses orthogonal rotation and produces a four-factor solution, while his colleague uses an oblique rotation that yields a three dimensional response. It is possible to determine how well one of the orthogonal factors is related to any of the oblique dimensions by establishing one of the configurations as the target and using factor comparison to intermesh the results.

These applications illustrate the general significance of CANONICAL ANALYSIS AND FACTOR COMPARISON—techniques that examine interrelationships and intermeshings of sets of variables.

—E. M. Uslaner, Series Editor

CANONICAL ANALYSIS AND FACTOR COMPARISON

MARK S. LEVINE
Research Department
Leo Burnett U.S.A.

INTRODUCTION

The purpose of this paper is to acquaint social scientists with some of the basic characteristics of the multivariate procedures that come under the general headings of canonical correlation and factor comparison. These are both umbrella labels in that they subsume a variety of related techniques, far more varied in the latter case than the former. One of the functions of this presentation will be to suggest certain of the alternatives available within each of the general headings. My style in presenting these techniques will be to emphasize the form of the research questions which these techniques can help illuminate and to identify the choices which the practicing researcher must be prepared to make in order to employ one or another of these methods of data analysis. I cannot hope to show the reader how, for example, to use *the* factor comparison techniques, since there are many techniques, each of which is appropriate to particular classes of research questions.

Since it is the editorial policy of this series not to present the full mathematical elaboration of the various statistical techniques covered in this and other volumes, my presentation will not include any systematic presentation of the various mathematical bases of many of these techniques. For the reader who has the appropriate skills, namely matrix algebra and

AUTHOR'S NOTE: *This paper was written while I was on the faculty of the Political Science Department of Northwestern University, Evanston, Illinois.*

calculus, the bibliography that I provide should enable him to fill in the deleted information. For several of the techniques discussed, computer software is commonly available to perform the calculations discussed. Since most of the procedures involve rather straightforward matrix manipulation, any reader with basic FORTRAN skills and access to a computing site with a matrix algebra subroutine package could easily implement the majority of the procedures to be discussed below if local routines are not available. Most of the authors of the methods discussed in this paper provide detailed information on appropriate computing algorithms for their techniques.

This literature is replete with a pattern of high density of cross-referencing and attention to the developments and innovations of others in this field. Perhaps it is that many of these techniques stem from the same seminal papers—the early papers of Hotelling (1935, 1936) and Bartlett (1941, 1948)—or the fact that most of the contributors to this literature are psychologists and thus read and contribute to the same journals, but the fact remains that there is a sense of cumulative advancement in the development of these techniques. On the other hand, despite this rather focused attention to the development of these techniques, there is considerable variety in the resultant methods of analysis. In certain of the cases to be discussed here, especially with respect to canonical correlation, there seem to be relatively few remaining puzzles to be solved. In the case of the factor comparison techniques, there are large numbers of solutions to essentially different puzzles and the data analyst must be alerted to the importance of the selection of the appropriate puzzle solution. Although this point should be obvious and unnecessary to state in print, the history of empirical social scientists selecting a conventional, convenient, and already programmed technique—such as principle components/varimax rotation, when that technique was suboptimal—suggests that I should make this point again.

For the reader who seeks a more (mathematically) complete presentation of the techniques to be discussed, there are several useful textbooks. Cooley and Lohnes (1971), Morrison (1967), Tatsuoka (1971), and Van de Geer (1971) all present informative discussions of canonical correctional analysis, each with unique emphases; Anderson's (1958) text is for the very brave. I have found no single adequate compilation of the various factor comparison techniques, although Rummel (1970) and, to a lesser extent, Harman (1967) contain some additional information. Basically the reader will have to go to the original papers which, happily, are concentrated in a few journals, *Psychometrika* most notably.

When originally solicited to write this paper, I was not at all clear why a discussion of canonical correlational analysis and factor comparison methods should be contained in the same paper, other than the fact that there might not be enough to say about either separately to fill this format. I have since concluded that there indeed good reasons to link these together if for no other reason than to clarify the fundamental differences between the questions to which each is appropriate. As a device to justify this paper and to give the reader an indication of the logic behind the organization of the presentation, consider the following data sets:

(1) Two sets of variables measured across the same units of observation at a point in time, that is, a standard subjects-by-variable cross-sectional data matrix divided vertically in half;

(2) One set of variables measured across the same units of observation at two points in time, that is, two temporally distinct cross-sectional matrices with identical row and column labels;

(3) One set of variables measured across two sets of units of observation at a point in time, that is, a single cross-sectional matrix divided in half horizontally.

These three classes of data sets are visually represented in Figure 1. Each of these three suggests a rather different class of data-descriptive research question:

(1) What can I say about one of these sets of attributes of these cases from knowledge of the other sets of attributes?

(2) How have these cases changed on these variables over time? Or, do the attributes of these cases go together in the same way now as they did then?

(3) Do the attributes of this set of cases go together in a different way than they do in that set of cases?

Canonical analysis is the method of choice for the first of these three data sets/research questions; factor comparison techniques for the third; and both techniques may help illuminate the second case which is the analysis of change data. My discussion will begin with a rather extensive introduction to canonical correlational analysis. Whereas it is possible to present a fairly exhaustive coverage of canonical within the format of this paper, a complete discussion of the range of factor comparison methods would require more space than available. Thus the discussion in that section will be limited to several of the more generally useful techniques.

A final point should be made to the reader regarding my expectations of his skills. Since I would hope that no one would consider employing the techniques discussed here without prior experience and understanding of multiple regression (for the canonical correlation discussion) and factor

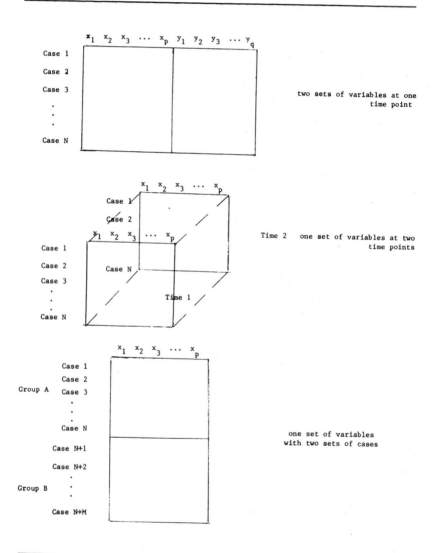

Figure 1: Various Configurations of Data to be Considered

analytic procedures (for the factor comparison portion), I will presume at least a knowledge of the basic characteristics of these techniques, that is, a level similar to the discussion of these techniques in such research methods books as Kerlinger (1973) or Leege and Francis (1974). I will employ as little mathematical notation as possible but will hope that the reader is at least familiar with such terms as "weighted sums," "orthogonality," and "communality." Other papers in this series, especially the introduction to factor analysis, may be useful to the beginning student of these methods. Where I do present more formal matrix formulae, they may be ignored by the reader without fear of missing any essential point.

I. CANONICAL CORRELATIONAL ANALYSIS

As is frequently demonstrated in multivariate textbooks, bivariate correlation and regression, multiple correlation and regression, and discriminant function analysis may all be treated as special cases of canonical correlation analysis. As a data reduction technique, canonical correlation in many ways subsumes factor analysis. Although the broad scope of this technique is of interest to the statistician, I am not suggesting that the reader replace his multiple regression program and its extensive auxiliary statistics with a canonical correlation routine. The unity of canonical correlation, and thus its appeal, lies in the questions it can help answer which the special-case procedures cannot optimally approach. Consider the situation in which the researcher is interested in explaining not one but several dependent variables by a set of independent variables. He seeks an explanation not of each of the dependent variables but rather *the set of dependent variables* taken together. Perhaps he is dealing with a multidimensional phenomenon like political participation or international conflict and is not interested in accounting for the variance of any one particular subconcept, but the concept as a whole. Using conventional multiple regression techniques, the usual approach would be to regress each dependent variable or index of each subconcept on the set of independent variables one at a time and in some arbitrary fashion combine the several results. There would be no opportunity to investigate the possibility that *combinations* of dependent variables relate to combinations of independent variables. It is specifically that capability of analyzing the relationships between sets of variables—many-to-many patterns of association as opposed to one-to-many patterns resulting from multiple regression—that makes canonical correlation a useful technique to political scientists. Whereas the movement from bivariate to multiple correlation and regression is, in some sense, a movement from simple (or simplistic) explanation to richer explanatory models, the shift from multiple regression to canonical correlation may facilitate the analysis of richer, that is, multidimensional, dependent variables. Not that performing canonical correlation will make a theory one bit better, but it may permit you to analyze crucial aspects of the theory which seemed intractable.

Let us assume that one has two sets of variables, conventionally a set of criterion or dependent variables and a set of predictor or independent variables. The imposition of this "causal" language is not central to the application of the techniques. The utilization of canonical correlational analysis can provide information concerning:

(1) the nature of the links or patterns of interdependency that join the two sets;

(2) the number of (statistically significant) links between the sets;

(3) the extent to which the variance in one set is conditional upon or redundant given the other set.

The ability to perform the redundancy analysis mentioned in the third point is debated, especially with regard to the appropriate statistical measure of redundancy. I will discuss several alternatives. The discussion of the first and second points is more straightforward although I will mention some unresolved issues and disputes as I go along. At this point our discussion will require some more formal mathematical notation which should not, however, be new to someone anticipating the use of canonical correlational analysis.

The Basic Canonical Correlation Model

Let us label our two sets of variables X and Y, which may or may not represent independent and dependent variable sets respectively. Each set is composed of several variables, $x_1, x_2, \ldots, x_p$, and $y_1, y_2, \ldots, y_q$, that is, there are p variables in the X set, q in the Y set. We have, then for each of the N units of observation its (p + q) scores on each of the variables in the X and Y sets, which can all be contained in a single partitioned data matrix as displayed in Figure 2. Each of the (p + q) variables is then intercorrelated with each of the remaining variables, producing a (p + q) by (p + q) square symmetric matrix of correlation coefficients.

As is conventional, I will assume that the coefficient computed is a Pearsonian product moment coefficient, r, although it seems reasonable to experiment with nonparametric associational statistics as the bivariate measures. Obviously, the choice of an alternative to Pearsonian r will make the notion of variance meaningless in subsequent portions of the analysis,

	x_1 x_2 x_3 $\cdots$ x_p	y_1 y_2 y_3 $\cdots$ y_q
Case 1		
Case 2		
Case 3	X SET	Y SET
.		
.		
.		
Case N		

Figure 2: Form of Data for Canonical Analysis

but I can see the utility of such a modification in exploratory analyses of a particular data set. The use of Pearsonian r obviously implies that the level of measurement of the data is interval, that is, equal differences in recorded scores represent equal differences in the possession of the measured trait, or that the analyst is prepared to assume that the data approximate interval properties. One must also assume that the *population* correlation and covariance matrices are positive definite, that is, that all principal diagonal minors are greater than zero. As Anderson (1958: 289) notes, one does not have to assume that the data are normally distributed but this assumption is necessary for the applicability of those tests of statistical significance which have been developed for the canonical correlational model. Finally there is the implicit assumption in this technique, and all the remaining techniques to be discussed in this paper, that the relationships among variables and sets of variables are *linear*. If the researcher postulates nonlinear dependencies, as in models with decreasing or increasing marginal returns to scale or threshold effects, then appropriate nonlinear transformations would have to be applied to the data to model such relationships within a linear computational routine. Introductory social statistics texts cover such procedures although econometrics textbooks tend to pay more attention to the problems of nonlinear relationships.

The matrix of correlations, R, can be partitioned into four submatrices. Rxx contains the correlations among the variables in the X set, Ryy the correlations among the Y set variables, and Rxy and Ryx the correlations of each of the variables in one set with each of the variables of the other set. By the symmetry property of a correlation matrix, we note that Rxy equals the transpose of Ryx, and vice versa. Thus we have two different types of information within R, the pattern of interdependencies within each of the sets and the pattern of correlations across the two sets. Figure 3 suggests the structure of R. Assuming that Rxy (or Ryx) contains at least some non-zero coefficients, the problem is then to determine the pattern of these between-sets correlations.

The analysis of this between-set pattern is accomplished by replacing the original variables in the X and Y sets by pairs of linear combinations of the original variables. We recall that a linear combination of variables is a weighted sum of those variables, therefore, if we have a set of variables $(z_1, z_2, z_3, \ldots, z_n)$, a linear combination of them, z, has the form:

$$z = a_1 z_1 + a_2 z_2 + a_3 z_3 \ldots + a_n z_n$$

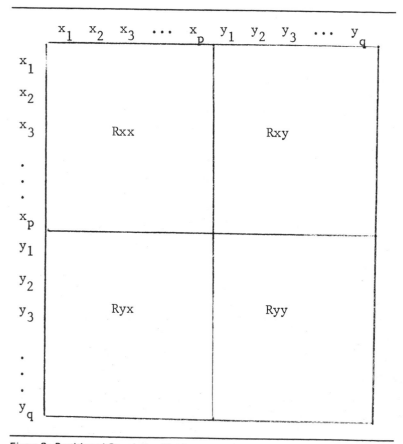

Figure 3: Partitioned Correlation Matrix

where $a_1, a_2, a_3, \ldots, a_n$ are constants. Using the more compact summation notation,

$$z = \sum_{i=1}^{N} a_i z_i$$

In canonical correlation analysis, a linear combination of the X variables is formed, as is a linear combination of the Y variables. Of the infinite number of possible linear combinations for each set, coefficients are chosen such that the resultant linear combination of the X set variables is maximally correlated with the linear combinations of the Y set variables. If we let $\underline{x}$ and $\underline{y}$ be defined by:

$$\underline{x} = \Sigma a_i x_i$$

$$\underline{y} = \Sigma b_i y_i$$

canonical correlation analysis selects those values for the a_i's and the b_i's such that $r_{\underline{x},\underline{y}}$ is the maximum possible value. Thus we can say that $\underline{x}$ represents that combination of the X set variables which has the highest correlation with *any* combination of the Y set variables and furthermore $\underline{y}$ is that combination of Y variables maximally correlated with *any* X combination. Of the infinite number of linear combinations of the two sets of variables we have found that particular pair most highly related to one another.[1] The correlation coefficient between $\underline{x}$ and $\underline{y}$ is termed a *canonical correlation*, r_c.

Having isolated $\underline{x}$ and $\underline{y}$, the job is not over. There is no assurance that there is only a single pair of linear combinations which are highly related to one another. Thus, $r_{\underline{x},\underline{y}}$ may be the maximum, but there may be other combinations, for example, $\underline{x}'$ and $\underline{y}'$, for which $r_{\underline{x}',\underline{y}'}$ is noticeably different from zero. Thus the next step is to locate that pair of linear combinations which have the second highest correlation. We constrain this next set of combinations to be uncorrelated with the first pair. The rationale here is that we want to identify statistically independent patterns of linkage between the sets.[2] If we did not impose this constraint, we could find an infinite number of combinations, each highly correlated with either $\underline{x}$ or $\underline{y}$, which would produce r_c's almost as high as the first. These combinations would, however, provide no new information about the between-set patterns, given the availability of $\underline{x}$ and $\underline{y}$. Again, having located the sets of coefficients, $a_1', a_2', \ldots, a_p'$, and $b_1', b_2', \ldots, b_q'$, that yield $\underline{x}'$ and $\underline{y}'$, we may continue to locate subsequent pairs of combinations, each pair necessarily having a smaller canonical correlation than the preceding pairs but the highest possible at its generation. All pairs produced after the first are constrained to be uncorrelated with all the preceding combinations. The nature of the mathematics involved in the procedures guarantees that there will never be more pairs than the number of variables in the smaller set, that is, there will be no more solutions than the minimum of (p,q).

To summarize these points, I will adopt the notation that $\underline{x}_1, \underline{y}_1$ are the first pair of linear combinations, which I will now call *canonical variates*; $\underline{x}_2, \underline{y}_2$ are the second pair of canonical variates, and so on. The conditions are:

$$\underline{x}_i = a_{i1} x_1 + a_{i2} x_2 + \ldots + a_{ip} x_p$$

$$\underline{y}_i = b_{i1} y_1 + b_{i2} y_2 + \ldots + b_{iq} y_q$$

Mean $(\underline{x}_i)$ = Mean $(\underline{y}_i)$ = 0, for all i.

Standard deviation $(\underline{x}_i)$ = Standard deviation $(\underline{y}_i)$ = 1.0
(usually, see below)

$$r_{\underline{x}_i,\underline{x}_j} = r_{\underline{y}_i,\underline{y}_j} = r_{\underline{x}_i,\underline{y}_j} = 0 \text{ if } i \neq j.$$

$r_{\underline{x}_i,\underline{y}_i}$ = Maximum across all possible sets of a's and b's given the orthogonality constraints.

The users of most canonical correlation programs should realize that the coefficients which are produced, the a's and b's, are coefficients to be applied to the original X and Y variables in standard-score form, that is, the X and Y variables transformed into z-scores. They are standardized weights which are expressed in a way that does not depend on the original scale of measurement and can be considered to indicate the direct contribution of each standardized variable to the total variance of the composite score. The application of these coefficients to the standardized X and Y variables will produce the canonical variate scores. These canonical variates will have means of zero, but their standard deviations depend on the particular way in which the computational algorithm scales the coefficients. This is a technical matter having to do with the underlying mathematics of the procedure.[3] Most computational routines will constrain the canonical variates to be standardized to have a mean of zero and a standard deviation of one. The reader is advised to check his local program on this since it is relevant to the computational of structural coefficients to be discussed later.

Let us assume that one has extracted all the (statistically significant) pairs of canonical variates linking the X and Y sets of variables. What one has done essentially is to replace the correlation matrix with which one started by the associated matrix of intercorrelations among canonical variates as presented in Figure 4. If s is the minimum of (p,q), then as stated by Morrison (1967: 215): "All the correlation between the sets of the original variates has been channeled through the s canonical correlations." Whatever linkage there was between the two sets, as manifested in the non-zero elements of Rxy, is captured by the s pairs of canonical variates and their interdependencies.

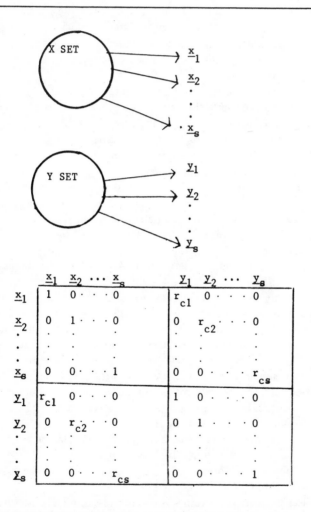

Figure 4: Schematic Diagram of Canonical Analysis

Interpretation of Canonical Variates

At this point the researcher has available several sets of information. He is informed that new variates, formed by the appropriate utilization of the weights produced by the algorithm and his original raw data in standardized form, contain all the between set interdependency originally in his data. He is informed as to the degree to which each pair of computed variates is correlated from the report of the canonical correlations. Yet his concern may well be to provide to himself and his potential audience the *content* of these new measures. If these new variates represent those particular linear combinations of the original variables which are most linked, what exactly is the nature (substantive content) of these new measures? One seeks, as in any procedure that extracts factors from a matrix, to interpret the results.

The obvious first suggestion on how to interpret the canonical variates is to look at what went into their composition. Specifically this would imply reviewing the matrix of weights, the a's and b's, which represent the direct contribution of each of the original variables to the composites. Although this seems an obvious suggestion, and indeed is made in several textbook presentations, it is one which is misleading and dangerous. The basic point is one which should be familiar to any researcher who has performed multiple regression with a battery of intercorrelated predictors. Multicollinearity, this condition of intercorrelated predictors, implies that the confidence intervals around the coefficients will be broad, that one variable may hide or suppress the importance of another variable correlated with the first, and a variety of other unpleasantries discussed by Darlington (1968) or any standard econometrics text. The suppression issue is probably the most crucial in the ability to interpret. What typically happens is that if two variables are closely correlated with each other, once one of the two has made its contribution to the composite, the other has no additional autonomous contribution to make. The first variable's coefficient will be high, the second's near-zero, that is, suppressed by the first. Now it is indeed true that these coefficients tell us how the variate is calculated, but I feel that it makes as much sense to try to interpret the content of the canonical variates from the regression coefficient matrix as to try to interpret the results of an orthogonal factor analysis by using the factor *score* coefficients. Since it is typically the case that the R_{xx} and R_{yy} matrices will contain some subsets of at least moderately intercorrelated variables, this critique of interpretation based on the matrix of weights will hold in the vast majority of cases.

If I reject the matrix of weights as a source of substantive interpretation of the canonical variates, I must present an alternative. The suggestion that

I present, along with Cooley and Lohnes (1971), Darlington et al. (1973), and Meredith (1964c), is that one interpret the content of the variates via the *correlations of the original variables with the canonical variate*. I am not concerned with what particular equation was used to generate the variate, but rather which of the original variables are highly correlated with it. This same approach is typically used in descriptive factor analysis where one describes the nature of the factors in terms of what cluster(s) of variables are empirically associated with the factor. The use of this approach to substantive interpretation recognizes that the composite is a manifestation of some abstract notion and information about the nature of this abstract phenomenon cannot be achieved directly—but can be acquired indirectly by asking what is related to it.

Following the terminology of Cooley and Lohnes (1971), I will refer to the matrix of correlations of the original variables of a given set with the canonical variates of that set as the canonical *structure* matrix, Sx or Sy. The matrices of weights will be A and B, for the X set and Y set, respectively. The matrices of canonical variates will be represented by $\underline{X}$ and $\underline{Y}$. A few simple matrix equations summarize some fundamental relationships. I assume that X and Y, the original variables, are in standard score form.

$\underline{X} = X\,A$	Post-multiplying the standard score data
$\underline{Y} = Y\,B$	matrices by the matrices of weights produces the canonical variate matrices.
$Sx = Rxx\,A$	One can obtain the structure matrix by pre-
$Sy = Ryy\,B$	multiplying the matrices of weights by the appropriate matrix of within-set correlations.

If the equations for calculating the structure matrices are to hold, the computational routine must be such that the resultant canonical variates are standardized. If such is not the case, then the preliminary coefficient matrices, A* and B*, reported by the computer program would have to be rescaled to give A and B.[4]

Perhaps the simplest method of calculating the structure matrix is to compute the canonical variate scores, which some programs do optionally or by the use of data transformation commands, such as COMPUTE cards in the SPSS environment. One then invokes a Pearson correlational routine to intercorrelate the canonical variate scores with the original data. Since to my knowledge none of the widely distributed canonical correlation routines—SPSS, BMD, Miami—produces the structure matrix, the researcher will have to either write his own coding to handle the simple matrix operations or compute the scores in order to backtrack to the structure matrix.

I specifically say that one *has* to do this since I firmly believe that as long as one wants information about the nature of the canonical correlational relationship, not merely the computation of the scores, one must have the structure matrix.[5]

Tests of Significance and Redundancy Analysis

To this point I have sidestepped the issue of statistical significance in canonical correlation analysis. The issue of significance in canonical analysis relates to the problem of the exact number of independent links that there are between the two sets of variables.[6] This is equivalent to asking how many pairs of variates have to be controlled to reduce the population interset correlation matrix, $\underline{R}$xy, to a zero matrix. As is typically the case with noisy data, that is, data which contains an error or random component in addition to the true score of the trait being measured, it will take the full number of solutions, that is, the minimum of (p,q), to reduce the *sample* Rxy to zero, but in the population fewer solutions might be required. Assuming that it is meaningful to talk about sampling and significance in one's research, there is a conventional test for determining the number of statistically significant solutions. This test can be broken into two steps. The first is a general test of whether there is *any* significant link between the sets, that is, whether there is at least one solution. Having passed this test, one then asks exactly how many significant solutions there are.[7]

The tests require the calculation of a simple statistic, V, by the formula:

$$V = \prod_{i=1}^{s} (1 - r_{ci}^2) = (1 - r_{c1}^2)(1 - r_{c2}^2) \ldots (1 - r_{cs}^2),$$

where s equals the minimum of (p,q). In a test given by Bartlett (1941), it is shown that under the null hypothesis that the sets X and Y are linearly unrelated, a particular function of V will be distributed approximately as a chi-squared variate. The test statistic, χ^2, is given by:

$$\chi^2 = - [N - .5\,(p + q + 1)] \ln V,$$

where N is the number of cases and ln denotes the natural logarithm function. Simple substitution shows that one can write the equation for χ^2 as:

$$\chi^2 = - [N - .5\,(p + q + 1)] \sum_{i=1}^{s} \ln (1 - r_{ci}^2)$$

χ^2 has (pq) degrees of freedom and its associated probability can be drawn from any standard tabulation of the chi-squared statistic. In Tatsuoka's (1971) text, some improvements on Bartlett's chi-square approximation are discussed. He cites corrections due to Schatzoff (1966) to make the Bartlett's test a better approximation of chi-square. An alternative function of V, which I will call F, due to Rao is also presented. The test statistic is:

$$F = \frac{1 - V^{1/t}}{V^{1/t}} \cdot \frac{mt - pq/2 + 1}{pq}$$

where $m = [N - .5 (p + q + 1)]$ and $t = [(p^2 q^2 - 4)/(p^2 + q^2 - 5)]^{\frac{1}{2}}$.

This statistic is distributed approximately as an F-ratio with (pq) and $(mt - pq/2 + 1)$ degrees of freedom. It is, according to Tatsuoka (1971: 88), "a closer approximate test." It is a somewhat more complex test to calculate, but the improvement in the approximation may well justify the slight inconvenience.

After having established that there is at least one significant linear relationship between the sets, one then becomes interested in identifying that number k, less than or equal to s, of significant solutions. The test used here operates incrementally. The test asks whether, having extracted one solution, there remains an additional significant solution; having extracted the second, is there a third. . . . After having extracted the first j solutions, let the statistic V_j be defined by:

$$V_j = \prod_{i=j+1}^{s} (1 - r_{ci}^2) = (1 - r_{c(j+1)}^2)(1 - r_{c(j+2)}^2) \ldots (1 - r_{cs}^2)$$

where, once again, s equals the minimum of (p,q). Note that $V_0 = V$ as defined above, so that this test is actually the general test of which the earlier test of total independence is a special case. One forms the test statistic χ_j^2, which is approximately chi-square distributed with $(p-j)(q-j)$ degrees of freedom:

$$\chi_j^2 = - [N - .5 (p + q + 1)] \ln V_j$$

$$= - [N - .5 (p + q + 1)] \sum_{i=j+1}^{s} \ln (1 - r_{ci}^2)$$

If this test is found to be significant, then one concludes that there are at least $(j+1)$ significant linear dependencies between the two sets. One calculates the sequence of values of χ_j^2 and notes the first insignificant result, let us say χ_u^2. Then we know that k, the number of significant solutions, equals u.

Having identified the number of linear dependencies between the sets and having information from the structure matrix of the content of these variates, a crucial issue remains: How much of the "variance" of the two sets is in common, or how much of the "variance" of the dependent variable set can be accounted for by the independent variable set? I enclose the word "variance" in quotation marks since there is no unequivocal definition of the notion of a *set*'s variance equivalent to the "mean sum of squared deviations" definition for a single variable. What one wants to have is a measure functionally equivalent to the squared (multiple) correlation coefficient, r^2 or R^2. It would be desirable to have such a measure not only for the entire set of k solutions—for example, how much of the Y set "variance" is captured by the set of k solutions—but also as a measure for each of the individual solutions. By this I mean that one wants to know how much of the two sets' "variance" is captured by the first pair of variates, compared to the second, and so forth. This information might easily be of more interest than the statistical significance of the solution; for example, there might be a significant link that accounts for a trivial amount of "variance." There are basically two traditions in the literature on approaching this problem, with no evidence that I have been able to find that the respective authors know of each other's existence, that is, there is no cross-referencing. I will present both and my preferences will become obvious.

The first approach to measuring the between-set overlap comes from Hooper (1959, 1962) and is discussed briefly by Theil (1971). Writing in *Econometrica*, Hooper (1959: 247) is concerned with a "complete system of linear stochastic relations" of the form:

$$Y B + X A = U$$

where the variables in the Y set are explicitly considered the jointly determined dependent variables and the X set the independent, explanatory variables. He develops a matrix generalization of the squared multiple correlation, linked to earlier developments of Hotelling and Wilks. The coefficient he suggests, $\bar{r}$, is termed the *trace coefficient* and is defined as the positive square root of $\bar{r}^2$:

$$\bar{r}^2 = 1/p \sum_{i=1}^{k} r_{ci}^2,$$

that is, the square root of the sum of the squared canonical correlations divided by the number of variables in the Y set. This easily calculable summary measure has received some attention in political science through its utilization by Rummel. The trace should be interpreted as the portion of the generalized variance of the dependent set accounted for by the systematic portion of the reduced form of the complete system of equations.[8] The trace ranges from zero to one, reaching its minimum value when Rxy is a zero matrix, its maximum when each of the Y variables is a linear combination of the X variables. Unfortunately, the interpretation of intermediate values is dependent on accepting and understanding Hooper's particular notion of generalized variance. Hooper presents some asymptotic sampling theory for the trace coefficient such that confidence intervals might be established. In the later article, he develops a notion of partial trace coefficients, perhaps best thought of as generalizations of multiple partial correlations (Cooley and Lohnes, 1971: 201-204). The trace coefficient is easy to calculate but difficult to interpret.[9]

The second tradition in the analysis of between-set overlap is based on the work of Stewart and Love (1968) and is extensively discussed in Cooley and Lohnes' (1971) text.[10] The development of what these authors call measures of *redundancy* is predicated on the fact that the canonical structure matrix—that is, the matrix of correlations of the original variables with the canonical variates—is a factor loading matrix. Obviously it is not the same factor loading matrix that one would obtain from a principal components analysis of the data, but it does contain the correlations of variables with orthogonal linear combinations of those variables. Let us assume that each original variable contributes one unit of variance to the set to which it belongs, the same assumption used in discussing variance in conventional factor analytic techniques. The amount of the total variance in the set accounted for by a factor is given by the sum of the squared loadings of the variables on that factor. That is, one asks what share of the total number of units of variance is captured in the factor and answers the question by squaring the elements of a column of the structure (or loading) matrix and summing. Since in canonical correlation analysis we are decomposing the sets into orthogonal linear combinations, we can calculate the shares of variance accounted for by each of the canonical variates and sum these together.

Of course the question we want answered in canonical correlation analysis is not how much of the variance in a set is captured by a variate from that set, but rather how much of the variance of a set as contained in the variate can be accounted for by a variate from the other set. We know that the canonical correlation is the conventional Pearsonian correlation between the variate from one set and the variate from the other set. Thus its square represents that proportion of the variance of one variate which overlaps the other. Combining these notions we find that the share of the variance of one set which can be accounted for by a canonical variate from the other set is equal to the product of the squared canonical correlation and the proportion of that set's variance contained in its variate. This rather complex and possibly ambiguous language is clarified diagramatically in Figure 5. One asks how redundant a set is, given the availability of information from the other set as contained in a canonical variate from that other set. One asks how much of the variance of the Y set variate is accounted for by the ith X set variate, r_{ci}^2, and what proportion of the Y set trace, V_{Yi}, is contained in the Y set variate. The multiplication of these two terms tells us that proportion of the Y set trace that is accounted for by the X set variate, therefore, how redundant the Y set is, given the X set variate.

Denote an element of the Y set structure matrix Syy by s_{ij}, with i ranging from 1 to k, the number of solutions, and j from 1 to q, the number of variables in the Y set. Let the percent of the Y set trace extracted by the ith Y set canonical variate, V_{Yi}, be defined as:

$$V_{Yi} = \frac{\sum\limits_{j=1}^{q} s_{ij}^2}{q}$$

Let the percent of the Y set trace accounted for by the ith X set canonical variate, that is the redundancy of the Y set given the ith solution, rd_{Yi}, be equal to:

$$rd_{Yi} = V_{Yi}\, r_{ci}^2.$$

The formulae for the X set redundancies are constructed in the same way.

I should emphasize that the redundancy coefficient is not symmetric. By this is meant that the share of the Y set trace accounted for by a particular variate from the X set is not equal, in general, to the share of the X set trace accounted for by the paired Y set variate. One can easily suggest

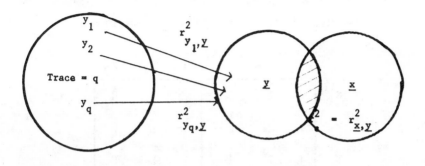

Figure 5: Schematic Diagram of Redundancy Analysis

an example in which, let us say, the first solution extracts a considerable share of the Y set trace—that is, most of the Y set variables load highly on the Y set variate—but has little of the X set trace, perhaps only one or two of the X set variables being associated with the X set variate. In such a case, assuming for the purpose of the example that the r_c^2 was high, the Y set would be highly redundant given the X set variate, but the reverse would not be true. Figure 6 suggests the form of this asymmetry. To use factor analytic terminology, a general factor of the Y set is accounted for by a specific factor of the X set. If one's research project is phrased in the language of dependent/independent sets of variables, then only one of two redundancy coefficients associated with each sequential solution need be calculated. Otherwise both should be reported since they may well vary noticeably.

One can summate the redundancy coefficients across the various solutions as a measure of the share of the total trace of one set accounted for by the several solutions. Since the variates are orthogonal, one can add up the individual pieces of the trace that the separate solutions extract into a measure of the total set variance accounted for by the solutions. As in factor analysis, one can calculate these sums cumulatively—that is, the percent of trace accounted for by the first solution, first and second solutions, and so forth, up to all solutions—as a device to determine how many of the solutions to retain for further consideration. Several other measures of redundancy are suggested by Darlington et al. (1973) but I suggest the Stewart-Love formulation as the most directly interpretable, given a "percent of the trace" notion of set variance, and relatively easy to calculate.[11]

Hypothetical correlation matrix

	x_1	x_2	x_3	y_1	y_2	y_3
x_1	1	L	L	H	H	H
x_2	L	1	L	L	L	L
x_3	L	L	1	L	L	L
y_1	H	L	L	1	H	H
y_2	H	L	L	H	1	H
y_3	H	L	L	H	H	1

Composition of canonical variates

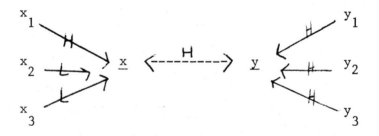

L = some very small value, e.g., nearly zero
H = some very large value, e.g., nearly one

Figure 6: Asymmetry of Redundancy Analysis

Some Illustrative Analyses

At this point a concrete worked example of an application of the canonical correlational method should help reify some of the issues I have presented. As is typical of examples presented to clarify methodological issues, I am not suggesting any substantive merit to the underlying hypothesis. The data were selected such that certain crucial points could be identified. The data are drawn from Taylor and Hudson (1970), the calculations performed in part through the SPSS canonical routine (Nie et al., 1970), with additional results calculated via the OMNITAB system (Hogben et al., 1971), all run on the Northwestern University CDC6400.[12]

The basic hypothesis or research question analyzed was the degree to which the distribution of expenditures within nations across various socially desirable activities could be accounted for by the basic socioeconomic and political characteristics of the nations. The dependent variables for the analysis were operationalized as the percentage shares of the total gross national product expended in the three areas of defense, education, and health. For the independent variables, I approximated a selection of variables from the dimensions previously identified by Russett (1967) of size, density ("intensive agriculture"), and economic development, with an additional variable suggesting political style. I chose three measures from the economic development cluster, that is, three measures which I had good reason to presume would be highly interdependent, to illustrate the effect of multicollinearity (non-zero correlations among the variables in a set) on the resultant matrices of weights. A second analysis to be reported here focused on a different dependent variable set, the distribution of the *sources* of GNP across agriculture, industry, and transportation/communications. Note that both of these demonstration analyses represent examples of the first type of data matrix and research problem discussed in the first section of this paper. A total of 12 variables were included in these runs and 58 nations had data across all the variables selected. Table 1 contains the mnemonic labels and definitions of the variables chosen. Table 2 contains the partitioned correlation matrix of the variables included in the first exercise.

As was expected, LIT, ENERGY, and GNP/POP are well correlated with each other and there are a variety of other moderate correlations within Rxx and Ryy. In Rxy one notes the substantial relationship between the economic development variables and the education expenditure variable, but clearly that might not be the only link worth identifying. Even in a rather simple 9 by 9 example, the complete multivariate pattern is difficult to "eyeball." Table 3 contains the preliminary results of the canonical correlational analysis of this matrix, preliminary in the sense

TABLE 1

Variables in the Demonstration Analyses

Mnemonic label	Variable description
Socio-eco-political variables	
POP	population size
DENS	population density
LIT	literacy rate
ENERGY	energy consumption per capita
GNP/POP	gross national product per capita
ELECT	electoral irregularity score
Expenditure distribution variables	
DEF	defense expenditure as a percent of GNP
EDUC	educational expenditure as a percent of GNP
HEALTH	health expenditure as a percent of GNP
Source of GNP variables	
AGRIC	percent of GNP from agriculture
INDUST	percent of GNP from industry
TRANS	percent of GNP from transportation and communication

that these results are what is likely to be reported by conventional canonical correlation routines.[13]

Ignoring for the moment the interpretation of the canonical variates, one notes that the first pair of canonical variates are correlated rather strongly, r_{c1} = .71; the second and third pairs are less so, r_{c2} = .49 and r_{c3} = .31. To the question of whether there is any statistically significant linear interdependency across the two sets, both the chi-squared test, χ^2_1, and the F test are highly significant. The chi-squared test suggests the statistical significance of the second solution, at the .05 level, but indicates that the third solution could have arisen by chance χ^2_3 (χ^2_3 = 5.83, df = 4, p > .1).[14]

In the matrices of weights is found the information necessary to calculate the three pairs of canonical variates from the original variables in standard score form. These coefficients indicate the direct contribution of each of the variables to the composite but may be quite misleading as indicators of the substantive content of the variates. In Table 4, I report the structure matrices for the two sets of variables, with associated statistics.[15] The comparison of the structure and weights matrices illustrates how easily one could be misinformed by the latter. Recall that the structure matrix indicates the correlation of the original variables with the canonical variates. All three of the economic development variables are highly correlated with the first X set variate, but in the matrix of weights one would be led to think that ENERGY has far less to do with the variate

TABLE 2
Bivariate Correlations for First Demonstration Analysis

	POP	DENS	LIT	ENERGY	GNP/POP	ELECT	DEF	EDUC	HEALTH
POP	1.00	.05	.20	.35	.33	.04	.38	.30	.13
DENS	.05	1.00	.45	.23	.19	.32	.03	.23	-.17
LIT	.20	.45	1.00	.71	.74	.36	.21	.61	.25
ENERGY	.35	.23	.71	1.00	.93	.19	.30	.64	.22
GNP/POP	.33	.19	.74	.93	1.00	.36	.33	.64	.15
ELECT	.04	.32	.36	.19	.36	1.00	.02	.17	.17
DEF	.38	.03	.21	.30	.33	.02	1.00	.27	-.02
EDUC	.30	.23	.61	.64	.64	.17	.27	1.00	.39
HEALTH	.13	-.17	.25	.22	.15	.17	-.02	.39	1.00

R_{xx} R_{xy}
R_{yx} R_{yy}

TABLE 3
Matrices of Weights and Related Statistics

	x_1	x_2	x_3
POP	-.24	.19	.81
DENS	-.04	-.90	.06
LIT	-.37	1.06	-.62
ENERGY	-.14	.91	-1.29
GNP/POP	-.49	-1.62	1.46
ELECT	.12	.23	-.35

	y_1	y_2	y_3
DEF	-.27	.14	1.00
EDUC	-.89	-.46	-.54
HEALTH	.01	1.10	.00

Solution	r_c	r_c^2	V	ln V	χ^2	df	prob
1	.71	.50	.34	-1.07	56.71	18	p<.001
2	.49	.24	.68	-.38	20.14	10	p<.05
3	.31	.10	.90	-.11	5.83	4	p>.1

$F = 3.40$ $df = (142, 18)$ $p<.005$

$\bar{r} = .53$

than either LIT or GNP/POP, less even than a variable outside this cluster, POP. Even the sign of the relationship of a variable and the canonical variate can be misjudged from its weight, as can be noted in the case of ELECT which has a positive weight in the equation for the first variate (.12) but is, in fact, negatively correlated with it (−.23). If one were to try to define the second canonical variate from the X set from the weights, one would "obviously" point to the economic development variables which have, in absolute value, the three highest coefficients. What is obviously the case from inspection of the structure matrix is that these three variables offset each other, GNP/POP's −1.62 contribution balancing LIT's 1.06 and ENERGY's .91, so that all three are basically uncorrelated with the composite variate. Even in the presence of very limited intercorrelation among variables in a set, as in the Y set, these problems arise. Note, for example, that the association of HEALTH with the first variate is only apparent in

TABLE 4
Structure Coefficients and Related Statistics

	x_1	x_2	x_3
POP	−.52	.12	.71
DENS	−.30	−.59	−.30
LIT	−.85	.04	−.39
ENERGY	−.92	−.03	−.15
GNP/POP	−.93	−.18	−.05
ELECT	−.23	−.55	−.24
Percent of trace	47.5	11.7	13.7

	y_1	y_2	y_3
DEF	−.52	.00	.86
EDUC	−.96	.01	−.27
HEALTH	−.34	.91	−.22
Percent of trace	43.7	28.0	28.3

Redundancy coefficients	Dependent set	
Solution	Y	X
1	.22	.24
2	.07	.03
3	.03	.01
Total	.32	.28

the structure matrix (b = .01, r = −.34), whereas on the second variate EDUC's seemingly large contribution distorts the fact that it is uncorrelated with that variate (b = −.46, r = .01). There are a variety of other comparisons that could be made—for example, compare DENSITY and ELECT on the second variate—but I think my point has been made: since the weights only indicate the direct contribution of the original variables to the calculation of the variate and since the effects of the correlations among the variables and the resultant indirect contributions may not be immediately apparent, the structure matrix is the only reasonable location to seek a substantive interpretation of the variates.[16]

As I have noted, the sum of the squared elements of a column in the structure matrix divided by the number of variables in the set is the proportion of the trace of the set captured in that variate. Recall here that a canonical variate is a factor of a matrix. Thus as in the conventional factor analysis case, one can identify the proportion of a set's "variance" associated with each solution, that is, 43.7 percent of the trace of the Y set and 47.5 percent of the X set are captured by the respective variates in the first solution extracted. As can be noted in this example, there is no assurance that these percents will monotonically decrease over the solutions. With these figures one can now calculate the redundancy coefficients for the two sets, both for each solution and the total sets of solutions. These figures suggest that 22 percent of the Y set trace is accounted for by the first X set variate. This conclusion seems intuitively clear in that the first Y set variate contains 43.7 percent of the Y set trace and that variate shares 50 percent of its variance with the first X set variate (r_{c1}^2 = .50). Over the three solutions, 32 percent of the Y set trace is accounted for. If the dependent/independent notion is irrelevant, one might also report that 28 percent of the X set trace is captured by the three solutions, noting as expected that the redundancy coefficients are not symmetric. For this example, the trace coefficient equals .53, which squared is .28. In this case the squared trace coefficient, which Hooper argues may be interpreted as the proportion of the jointly determined set's variance accounted for by the reduced form model, is roughly equal to the summed redundancy measure for the Y set, .32 vs. 28. The availability of the solution-by-solution redundancy coefficients should raise the question of the significance of the various solutions, specifically whether the statistically significant second solution is worth further attention. I presume that it is somewhat a matter of taste whether one pays attention to a seven percent chunk of the Y set, whether or not significant in a statistical sense. It is clear that scientific, substantive importance and statistical significance are not identical concepts, although they are often naively confused.

Table 5 reports the structure matrices from a second run with different Y set variables, the X set unchanged. This example is included to make one simple point: the canonical variates extracted from a set of variables are not, in general, invariant as one varies the composition of the other set. Although there is some similarity between this matrix and the one reported earlier, they are clearly not identical. The canonical variates extracted from X are dependent on the nature of Y and the XY relationships. If you change Y, you will in general change the composition of the X set variates.

TABLE 5
Structure Coefficients, Alternative Y Set Variables

	x_1'	x_2'	x_3'
POP	-.19	-.10	.05
DENS	-.31	.21	-.73
LIT	-.77	.39	-.30
ENERGY	-.86	.35	.11
GNP/POP	-.73	.60	.22
ELECT	.17	.86	-.40
Percent of trace	33.7	23.5	14.0

	y_1'	y_2'	y_3'
AGRIC	.74	-.68	.04
INDUST	-.99	-.12	.03
TRANS	-.05	.56	.82
Percent of trace	50.7	26.3	22.7
r_c	.85	.67	.22

This lack of uniqueness of the canonical variates is one of the reasons I find it hard to conceptualize the utilization of the canonical variate *scores*— that is, the values each case obtains on the composite measure—in subsequent analyses. These scores are not unconditional attributes of the sets, but are rather conditional, jointly determined results. I presume one could construct a research design in which one had, let us say, an independent variable set of those combinations of expenditures best predictable from socioeconomic characteristics, that is, the Y set canonical variates. The theory which might motivate the utilization of such variables is far more subtle than I am comfortable with. One might calculate the canonical variates for the two sets and regress the Y set variates on the X set variate, as suggested by Phillips (n.d.) as a means for detecting those cases for which the residuals were great, namely those cases for which the general relationship seems not to hold.

Some Additional Topics

Having presented this worked example, there remain a few issues to be raised and some extensions of the technique to be mentioned. The first issue is whether one should perform a preliminary orthogonalization (a principle components analysis) of each of the two original sets of data prior to the canonical analysis, then submitting the two sets of factor scores to canonical correlation analysis. Clearly such a first step would eliminate the problems of the difference of the weight and structure matrix, since in the case of orthogonal variables the two matrices are identical. I would, however, not suggest this as a general strategy since one tends to lose the identifiable content of the original variables in the orthogonal composite. The canonical variates in such a case would be composites of composites, making substantive interpretation extraordinarily difficult. Only in the case of a researcher who lacks programming skills and therefore cannot compute the structure matrix might I suggest this approach.[17]

I have avoided discussion of missing data in the presentation for the simple reason that there is really nothing new to say about it. The literature I reviewed literally does not mention missing data in canonical analysis.[18] The effect of missing data on the extraction of and characteristics of eigenvalues is discussed by Rummel (1970: 259-261) in the context of factor analysis, but the exact implication of missing data on the estimates of the various canonical statistics has not been addressed. Clearly any of the conventional responses to missing data can be suggested: deleting cases with missing data, calculating each individual correlation on the basis of cases which have data on both variables, substituting the mean for missing data, or using a regression equation to estimate missing values. I know of no formal or numerical (Monte Carlo) study of the merits of one or another technique in canonical analysis. At least with respect to the first two alternatives, the SPSS listwise versus pairwise distinction, I would run my data both ways given available computer resources. The choice between these two alternatives may greatly encroach on any claims of generalizability and reliability of one's findings. As a simple demonstration of the variance in results possible through choice of a missing data option, consider the results in Table 6. I simply repeated the analysis of the variables in the first example, but changed to a pairwise deletion of missing data. If one compares the structure matrices in this table to the earlier results in Table 4, the differences are apparent. Whereas in the earlier run the first variate in the Y set might be viewed as a general factor—that is, all variables in the set correlated with it—no such variate appears clearly in this reanalysis.[19] The second variate in this analysis is

TABLE 6
Structure Coefficients, Pairwise Deletion Option

	x_1	x_2	x_3
POP	.06	.03	−.40
DENS	.95	.00	−.14
LIT	.07	.85	−.13
ENERGY	−.06	.88	−.26
GNP/POP	−.06	.83	−.48
ELECT	−.24	.07	−.65
Percent of trace	16.2	36.7	15.3
	y_1	y_2	y_3
DEF	.99	.10	.04
EDUC	.06	.99	−.14
HEALTH	.03	.39	.92
Percent of trace	33.1	38.0	28.9
r_c	.78	.45	.19

the closest to a general factor in this run and the loading of DEF on it is marginal. Even the between-set interdependencies may vary as noted in comparing the results for the second Y set variate in the earlier run to the third one in the current analysis. Both variates are virtually exclusively defined by HEALTH, but the paired X set variates differ considerably in content; the earlier one is defined by DENS and ELECT, while the current variate is defined by ELECT, GNP/POP, and POP. My only advice is that the analyst explore the possible effects of the choice of response to missing data via reanalyses.

Even if one does not have missing data, one's data may well be unreliable; for example, there may be an error component in the measures one has obtained. The classical development of the canonical correlation model assumes no such noise in the data, but social scientists operating in a psychometric tradition often are concerned with reducing the effect of data unreliability. Several approaches to this problem have been suggested. Meredith's (1964c) early approach is rather complicated and, as argued by Darlington et al. (1973), gives the same results as a simpler strategy. Their suggestion is to introduce the conventional correction-for-attenuation formula and adjust each element of the original correlation matrix on the basis of the reliabilities of the variables being correlated. This implies dividing each correlation by the square root of the product of the two reliability estimates. Since reliability estimates are always less than or equal to unity, this correction implies an upward shift in the values of the correlations. Van de Geer (1971) provides an alternative of using the reduced correlation matrices, that is, the original Rxx and Ryy with estimates of the reliability of each variable on the diagonal. Whereas the Darlington suggestion involves the rescaling of the off-diagonal elements of the correlation matrix, the Van de Geer approach operates on the diagonal of that matrix, leaving the off-diagonal elements alone.[20] There seems no assurance that these two methods will exactly converge, nor a clear argument for choosing one or the other. My preference is the Darlington method since it does not affect the trace of the matrix and thus should not interfere with redundancy analysis as developed earlier. Both procedures will tend to produce a greater number of statistically significant solutions and the analyst is cautioned to check for substantive interpretability.

Several extensions of canonical correlation analysis have been suggested. Hall (1969) discusses the rotation of canonical variates to assist interpretation. Cooley and Lohnes (1971) allude to a notion of partial canonical correlation in which both X and Y set variables are first regressed on some other variable(s), let us say Z. The residuals from these regressions are calculated and the two sets of residuals are then canonically correlated.[21] Horst (1961a,b) presents a variety of models and an iterative estimation procedure for the extension of canonical correlation analysis to more than two groups of variables. Thus instead of identifying the linear patterns linking X and Y, one seeks patterns linking X, Y, Z. Tucker's (1958) interbattery factor analysis is often mentioned as an alternative to canonical analysis. Tucker presents his method in the context of cross-battery replication and reliability, an important issue; but as is shown by Darlington et al. (1973), the hypothesis tested by Tucker's method is the same as that tested in canonical analysis. Their conclusion is that since canonical has tests of significance while the Tucker procedure does not, the former should be the method of choice.

II. FACTOR COMPARISON TECHNIQUES

In the discussion of canonical correlational analysis, the data matrix under analysis was composed of two distinct sets of variables, measured on the same units of observation. In this section, I will consider the situation in which one has the same set of variables measured either on two different sets of units of observation or on the same set of units but at two different points in time. Whereas in the previous discussion the form of the research question being posed took the shape of identifying the pattern of linear interdependencies linking the two sets of variables, the questions under consideration now take the form of inquiring whether the same structure of interdependencies within a set of variables characterizes two different groups of cases or the same group of cases at two different times. One might be asking whether the way in which political attitudes cluster together for subjects drawn from the population of the United States is the same or different from the way that characterizes a sample drawn from Yugoslavia.[22] One might be interested in the convergence or divergence of the patterns of interdependencies among socioeconomic characteristics of nations in 1965 as opposed to 1950. It should be obvious that the issues of stimulus equivalence or comparability are central to any such comparative analysis, whether comparison be across space or time. There are a variety of subtle epistemological issues which should be considered by a researcher in the development of a design calling for these methods of comparison and a careful reading of Przeworski and Teune (1970) is advised.

Target Analysis

Within the general discussion of factor comparison techniques, a particular special case should be identified. While I have stated that these techniques compare structures derived from two different data sets, there is the important case in which one of the two structures being compared is not an empirically determined structure, but rather a theoretically hypothesized structure. Consider the situation where one postulates that, for some particular class of subjects, responses to questions tapping sense of personal efficacy would correlate with each other but not with measures of alienation, and neither efficacy nor alienation responses would cluster with political participation measures. In such a case, one might test this set of related hypotheses by recognizing that one was implicitly predicting that, should one factor analyze these three sets of measures simultaneously, one would expect to obtain a factor solution in which efficacy items load on factor(s) on which neither alienation nor participation items load, alienation items load on "pure" alienation factors, and the same for partic33ipation. In other words, one's hypotheses make predictions about the structure of the resultant factor matrix. One could then construct this hypothesized, or *target* matrix, and compare one's empirically determined factor matrix with the target. One is trying to confirm or disconfirm a particular previously specified prediction about the multivariate properties of one's data.

It is my personal preference, for a broad variety of hypotheses which might be tested via such target analysis, to use the more powerful techniques of canonical analysis. The particular example provided could be more readily approached by positing no significant canonical correlations linking any pair of the three sets of variables. Hypothesizing that two sets of variables should load together would be equivalent to predicting high canonical correlations linking the sets. Especially since canonical gives a broader set of additional diagnostically useful statistics and tests of significance, I typically advise it as the method of choice over target analysis. The development of Jöreskog's methods, to be discussed later, should also help to reduce the utilization of target procedures. Since, however, target analysis is reported occasionally in the social science literature and since it provides a convenient introduction to factor comparison techniques, I will discuss it here.[23]

All but one of the factor comparison techniques mentioned in this section are based on the notion of a transformation of a given matrix so that the matrix after transformation fits in some sense, usually least squares, another matrix. The same logic underlies regression analysis in that one locates a transformation which when applied to the independent variables produces a result, the predicted values of the dependent variable, which best fits the dependent variable. Algebraically, one finds a matrix of regression coefficients, B, which minimizes the sum of the squared elements of the error vector, E, in the matrix equation $Y = X B + E$. B transforms X in a way that minimizes the criterion of least squared errors. Basically the same logic prevails in matrix comparison techniques. I will assume that there are two factor matrices of interest, the target F and the empirically determined result F_1.[24] For a variety of reasons, such as the type of rotation chosen, F and F_1 might differ even to the extent of having different numbers of columns. One then finds that transformation matrix, T, that when applied to F_1 produces the closest fit to the target F. In matrix equations, the general model is $F = F_1 T + E$ where E is the matrix of errors of fit and the matrix $F^* = F_1 T$ is the resultant transformation of the original matrix.

There are essentially two general approaches to this kind of target analysis, both of which are based on the same model, $F = F_1 T + E$. The two approaches differ in the restrictions placed on the transformation that may be applied to the matrix F_1 to rotate it toward F. In the tradition that begins with Ahmavaara's work (1954a,b), followed by the writings of Hurley and Cattell (1962), and is extremely well presented by Rummel (1970), the transformation matrix will usually not be orthogonal. The implication of this is that while prior to transformation the factors defined in F_1 may have been orthogonal, after rotation to best fit with the target, the factors of F* will not be orthogonal. In the alternative "orthogonal Procrustes" tradition, based on the work of Green (1952), Schonemann (1966), and Cliff (1966), restrictions are imposed on the transformation matrix so that the factors, if orthogonal prior to target rotation, are orthogonal in F*.[25] This restriction on the transformation is occasionally labeled *rigid* rotation. The choice between these two assumptions must be predicated on the development within one's research design of a notion of the meaning of comparison and the freedom that one is prepared to allow in the computational procedures to achieve good fit. There are very strong arguments for preference of nonrigid rotation if one is comparing two empirically based results, but these arguments may not hold for target analysis as a hypothesis testing procedure.[26] I do not have a clear preference between these procedures and must leave it to the researcher to consider the implications of choosing one or the other. For the analyst in an OSIRIS environment, the issue is less threatening in some sense since experimentation with both procedures is feasible through routines FCOMP (Ahmavaara) and COMPARE (orthogonal Procrustes). The ability to experiment with methodological alternatives does not, however, obviate the need to make the final choice among methods on a theory-consistency basis.

Should one not have access to a target comparison routine, the programming required is rather straightforward in either approach. The Ahmavaara transformation matrix, T_A, is produced by solving the matrix equation:

$$T_A = (F_1' F_1)^{-1}(F_1' F)$$

where F_1' is the transpose of the original empirical factor matrix and F is the target. Since most computing facilities have subroutines to perform matrix inversion and multiplication, most of the required coding would be simple input/output commands. The orthogonal Procrustes approach is somewhat more complicated, requiring the extraction of the eigenvectors of certain matrices, but again standard eigenproblem routines are usually available. The procedure is to form a matrix, A,

$$A = F_1' F$$

and extract the eigenvectors of the matrices $A'A$ and AA', M and N respectively, from the equations:

$$A'A = MDM'$$
$$AA' = NDN'$$

where D is the diagonal matrix of eigenvalues. Note that the eigenvalues of $A'A$ and AA' are the same. The orthogonal Procrustes transformation matrix, T_0, is given by:

$$T_0 = NM'.$$

Since the orientations of the eigenvectors are arbitrary, one may have to reflect some of them to obtain the final solution. Schonemann (1966) gives explicit instructions on an appropriate computing algorithm. Having calculated either of the two transformation matrices, one then postmultiplies the original empirical factor matrix by the transformation matrix to get the rotated result which best fits the target matrix, $F^* = F_1 T$.[27] One can then calculate the matrix of errors, $E = F - F^*$, and potentially isolate those variables or those factors which come into best (or worst) alignment with the target. One should note that neither of these techniques presumes necessarily equal number of factors, that is, the number of columns, in each of the matrices compared.

There have been some modifications and elaborations of these techniques from their original formulations. Browne and Kristof (1969) provide a model similar to Ahmavaara's which assumes that the factor scores have equal variances in the target population and in the empirical sample. Computationally their technique is more complex than the original and the assumption concerning factor score variance seems unnecessary. The most important modification of the original orthogonal Procrustes notions has been Schonemann and Carroll's (1970) extension which permits the target and empirical matrices to have different scales and origins. As they note, this method would be suited to comparison of structures extracted under different scaling procedures, for example, factor analysis versus multidimensional scaling. It is this most recent routine which is contained in the OSIRIS program COMPARE. For most target applications, one should assume that no rescaling nor translation of origin is required and these options should be suppressed.

There is an important epistemological issue which should be mentioned in the context of target analysis. It is suggested in the name that Hurley and Cattell (1962: 260) gave to one of their early programs. Procrustes was one "whose beds fitted all travelers. Those who were too short for his beds he cruelly stretched, and those who were too tall he cut down to size." As has been noted by Overall (1974), target analysis tries to confirm a particular hypothesis rather than to falsify it. Conventionally most readers would not be happy with a researcher who claims the validity for his hypothesis after having forced his data to fit his hypothesis. In some way, such target rotation forces one's empirical data to fit the target and thus "this program lends itself to the brutal feat of making almost any data fit almost any hypothesis" (Hurley and Cattell, 1962: 260). Especially since tests of significance are not well developed for these analyses—that is, tests of the degree to which the forced fit is any better than one could have obtained by forcing any data to the target—I advise cautious applications of these methods. This confirmation bias is one of the strongest reasons I have for the preference of canonical analyses over target procedures whenever possible.

Schonemann and Carroll (1970) provide some discussion of measures that might be used to measure the degree of fit to a target matrix. Rummel (1970) suggests correlating the elements of F and F*, and there are other measures to be discussed below which might be useful in identifying which factors come into closest alignment with the target. There is not, however, anything resembling sufficient knowledge of the sampling distribution of these measures to provide a nonsubjective decision rule. Although it is feasible to compare degrees of fit—that is, determining which alternative target matrix an expirical matrix fits best, by comparing statistics like the sum of squared errors—one still has no information concerning the significance of any of the fits. There have been some limited Monte Carlo studies, such as Cattell et al. (1969) and Nesselroade and Baltes (1970), which may be used to suggest some guidelines, but there remains an unavoidably large amount of subjectivity in any discussion of the goodness of fit. This absence of tests of significance and the implicit bias towards confirmation makes me suggest extreme caution in the utilization of these techniques.

A factor analysis procedure has been developed which, once the computer software becomes better developed and more widely distributed, may eliminate virtually any need for target routines as a device for testing fit to a hypothesized matrix. The work of Jöreskog (1966, 1969; Jöreskog and Lawley, 1968) includes the development of what is termed confirmatory maximum likelihood factor analysis. In this method one has the option of predetermining certain attributes of the final results. Specifically one can specify some or all of the elements of the factor pattern matrix; some or all of the communalities can be predetermined; some or all of the elements of the interfactor correlation matrix can be given. The procedure then chooses values for those parameters that have been left free to vary in a way that best fits the predetermined parameters. One could, for example, predetermine the composition of several factors and let the remaining factors be located in a way determined solely by one's data.

Having produced those values for the free terms which best suit the requisites of the model, a chi-square test is available which evaluates whether the factors so extracted sufficiently reduce the original covariance structure. Additionally the procedure provides approximate tests of significance on the estimated values, that is, the values left free to vary. If there is a major weakness in this method, it is that the technique does not yield a unique solution unless one has prespecified a sufficient number of appropriately placed parameters. Usually, however, one should have an explicit enough hypothesis about the results that sufficient parameters can be specified to yield a unique solution. The other difficulty with the procedure is its limited availability in standard packages. Programs, of which LISREL is the most recent, are distributed by the Educational Testing Service for these purposes, but many computing centers do not have these routines. Thus my suggestion of the potency of this technique is based on its formal characteristics as shown in the articles cited, not on the basis of personal experience in using the technique. Thus I suggest that the reader investigate this technique and the availability of software, but I cannot recommend its adoption as a proven alternative to the other procedures discussed.

Factor Matrix Comparisons

Whereas in target analysis I have assumed that the researcher is comparing a single empirical matrix to a target, it is easy to think of situations in which one is interested in the comparability of two empirical matrices. One might be asking whether, aside from the idiosyncracies of the particular final rotation employed in two separate factor analyses, the two final matrices indicate a similar pattern of interdependency among the variables. One realizes that there are a variety of reasons why two matrices might look dissimilar while there might be a simple rotation of each that would bring them into (near) perfect alignment. One is asking whether the "same" factor emerges in various data sets, whether its presence can be replicated in various contexts. I am not, by very conscious choice, going to open up the Pandora's box of "can one truly discover anything via the factor machine?" I will presume that the researcher who considers performing factor comparisons has made the decision that a factor is something more than a statistical result and can justify the comparison of factor structures.

The motivation for factor matrix comparisons is often that suggested by Cattell and Baggeley (1960: 33): "A factor once found remains merely a hypothesis about a pattern; it is verified only after the pattern has been found again in well-defined circumstances." Another motivation which does not hinge on the discovery interpretation of factor analysis might be to assess the effect of some classificatory variable such as race or sex on the multivariate pattern or interdependencies among a set of measures. Whatever the motivation, I will assume that one has obtained two empirical factor matrices, F_1 and F_2, based on data from two different groups of cases or two different subsamples of a single population, the similarity of which one wants to assess. Before I present some of the techniques for performing such comparison, there are several issues that must be raised.

If one has access to the raw data for the two groups of cases, it might be useful to pool the two matrices, adding a dummy variable indicating group membership. The loading of this identification variable would indicate those factors, assumed to exist in both groups, on which the groups are most discriminated, therefore, the factors for which the groups' mean factor scores would be most different. This procedure can be extended to cover more than two groups by proper scoring of a set of dummy variables. This technique, of course, does not give separate factor structures for the two groups but, in the Przeworski and Teune (1970) tradition, one should always assume that the cases from two or more groups are homogeneous until this assumption breaks down empirically. In the case where one does not have all the original data—for example, if one is comparing one's own data to another previously published study, the data from which is not available—this suggestion cannot be implemented.

Rummel (1970) argues that the variety of preliminary decisions made in the course of factor analysis be the same across the two or more studies being compared. He argues for utilization of the same scaling procedures on the original data, associational statistic and factor extraction procedures to ensure that the degree of dissimilarity between studies can be attributed to differences in interdependencies, not differences in methods. Some violation of these principles can be absorbed; for example, the Schonemann/Carroll procedure might be used to rescale and reposition the factor matrices. As a general rule, comparability of procedures removes one obvious plausible rival source of variance.

Another issue provoked by Rummel is what can be compared across factor analytic studies. Although I will focus on the comparison of factor loading matrices, Rummel mentions several other statistical results produced in the course of a factor analytic study which either could be or should be compared. In the limiting case, anything that varies across occasions or objects can be compared and thus I should not want to exclude the comparison, let us say, of the standard deviations of the factor score coefficients. What is meaningless to me may be a critical test to you. On the other hand, as Rummel suggests, there are several results the comparison of which may provide substantive information. In his discussion (1970: 450-453), he suggests the comparison of the loadings, the complexity or simplicity of the structure, the variance accounted for by each and all of the factors, the communalities, and the number of significant factors. He also points out that each of the matrices produced in factor studies, from the inverse of the correlation matrix to the factor score matrix, has content that can be explored. If one were arguing, for example, that ideologues will have a more patterned and cohesive set of political attitudes than individuals without strong ideological commitments, I might suggest that this hypothesis be converted into the expectation that a factor analysis of a battery of political attitudinal items administered to these two groups would have fewer factors (that is, greater cohesion) and a higher percent of variance accounted for (that is, greater pattern) in the ideologue group.

Factor Loading Matrices

I will focus the remaining discussion on the comparison of factor loading matrices but immediately must raise still another issue, that of whether one should compare entire matrices or columns drawn from different matrices. This is the distinction between matrix and vector comparisons in Rummel's terminology. As he says (1970: 463): "The difficulty with the vector comparison approach is that the factors are compared as given. Exogenous influences may affect the independent rotations of two studies and confound the comparisons." But one might argue that this difficulty with vector comparisons, that is, the comparison of the loadings of a set of variables exactly as they came off the print-out, is in some sense a strength. Given the bias toward confirmation of similarity that any convergence rotation would imply, one might prefer the more strenuous test that the variables load in an invariant way without adjustments.

There is the additional question of how much of several matrices one should expect to converge. In an important recent article, Please (1973) develops a model in which one assumes that there are factors common to all subgroups and other subgroup-specific factors. In this not unreasonable situation, the application of a matrix transformation designed to bring the matrices into maximal congruence might very well under-fit the true across-groups common space and over-fit the group-specific unique spaces. Since, for example, in the case of least squares rotations like Ahmavaara's, the last factor contributes as much as the first factor to the total adjustment, I would carefully consider the full implications before rotating to convergence. Again, given that much of this is a matter of style and preferences, I will present both vector and matrix techniques.

Several of the obvious candidates for indices of vector similarity are reviewed by Harman (1967), Rummel (1970), and Pinneau and Newhouse (1964). One could compute the correlations between the loadings of a set of variables across two studies. Indeed, if one had found $\underline{m}$ factors which comprised F_1 and $\underline{n}$ factors in F_2, then one could compute the $\underline{m} \times \underline{n}$ matrix of correlations, matching each of the factors of F_1 with each of those in F_2, although the risk of finding matches due only to chance increases greatly. These correlations would indicate the extent to which there were factors in the studies on which variables loaded in a proportionally equal fashion. Thus although a factor in one study might have many variables strongly loading on it and a factor in the other study might have very weak loadings, the loadings could still be perfectly correlated, that is, the pattern of *relative* high and low loadings be identical.

If one considers differences in the magnitude of loadings to be important as well as differences in the pattern, one can use the root mean square measure, RMS, defined as the square root of the average squared difference of the loadings of the variables. Let f_1 and f_2 be columns of F_1 and F_2, respectively, where f_{1i} and f_{2i} are the loadings of the ith variable on these two factors. Then the formula for RMS is:

$$RMS = \left[\frac{\sum_{i=1}^{k} (f_{1i} - f_{2i})^2}{k} \right]^{1/2}$$

where k is the number of variables in the two studies. This coefficient imposes the most severe comparison since deviation in either patterns or magnitude will be picked up. RMS reaches a minimum of zero, for a perfect pattern-magnitude match and a maximum of two, when all loadings are equal to unity but of opposite signs across studies. Intermediate values, for example, one, are difficult to interpret in terms of goodness of fit.

A more well-behaved measure that is sensitive to both pattern and magnitude differences is the coefficient of congruence, CC, suggested by Wrigley and Neuhaus (1955). Its formula is:

$$CC = \frac{\sum_{i=1}^{k} f_{1i} f_{2i}}{\left[\left(\sum_{i=1}^{k} f_{1i}^2 \right) \left(\sum_{i=1}^{k} f_{2i}^2 \right) \right]^{1/2}}$$

that is, the sum of the products of the paired loadings divided by the square root of the product of the two sums of squared loadings. This is not a correlation coefficient since the two sets of loadings are not standardized. Although this coefficient is widely used, it has been repeatedly noted that one gets a high CC whenever two factors have many variables with the same algebraic sign.

Like RMS, the sampling distribution of CC is not known, precluding tests of significance of matches. Further, in my estimation the fact that RMS and CC are sensitive to both pattern and magnitude is not a desirable trait. My preference, as a general principle, is to construct indicators that tap single unidimensional domains of content. I can always combine unidimensional measures but I cannot usually break a single number into its several parts. Further in the tradition of Cattell's (1944) parallel proportional profiles, I would argue that pattern similarity is the crucial issue. The question in factor comparison seems to be whether variables cluster together or are similarly interrelated in several groups of cases. The underlying factor variate, that construct the existence of which one is probing in different settings, might have more or less variance across groups. If it has less variance, then the variables sensitive to it would be expected to have less systematic variance, and thus would be expected to have low communalities. But despite their low loadings, one would expect these variables to load with exactly the same pattern as in situations in which the underlying variate has high variance.[28]

This line of thinking is contained in the development of Cattell's salient variable similarity index, S, as presented in Cattell et al. (1969) and Cattell and Baggaley (1960). The computation of this index is based on the classification of loadings into salient and hyperplane categories. A hyperplane loading may be operationally defined as a near-zero loading, usually taken to mean a loading in the range from −.1 to +.1. Loadings in excess, in absolute value, of .1, or some other cutoff value, are considered to indicate variables salient to the factor, in Cattell's sense variables on which the underlying factor is acting.[29] Variables lying in the hyperplane of a factor have a relationship to that factor no greater than expected by chance. The salient loading variables are further categorized as positive or negative salients according to their algebraic sign. Thus the loadings of a set of variables on the factors being compared can be expressed in a 3 by 3 table, with the categories being positive and negative salients and hyperplane. The index S is calculated from this cross-tabulation by comparing the various cell frequencies. (See Figure 7 for the cell structure.) The index is calculated as:

$$S = \frac{c_{11} + c_{33} - c_{13} - c_{31}}{c_{11} + c_{33} + c_{13} + c_{31} + .5\,(c_{12} + c_{21} + c_{23} + c_{32})}$$

The index may be seen as a comparison of the difference between the number of hits and misses as a proportion of a weighted sum of the cell frequencies; S will reach a maximum value of unity when there is a perfect match, a minimum of minus one for a perfect match with one of the factors reflected, and zero when there is no congruence. It is, thus, a well behaved statistic. This measure is extremely simple to calculate and has a distinct intuitive sensibility to it. Of course, the index is throwing out a large amount of the available data, that is, it equates a loading of .9 with one of .3. It reduces the factor loadings to an ordinal measure but while there is a loss of information, there is also a lessened risk of capitalizing on chance differences among the loadings. On the other hand, S can be capricious, linking strongly factors whose similarity might seem marginal.

Although the theory of the sampling distribution of S is not known, one has the results of an extensive Monte Carlo study of the empirical distribution of S under the assumption of unrelated factors (Cattell et al.,

	PS	HY	NS
PS	c_{11}	c_{12}	c_{13}
HY	c_{21}	c_{22}	c_{23}
NS	c_{31}	c_{32}	c_{33}

PS = positive salient

HY = hyperplane

NS = negative salient

Figure 7: Cell Labels for Calculation of Cattell's S

1969). In a series of tables, one finds the empirical cumulative distribution and probability levels of S for varying combinations of numbers of variables and proportion of the variables lying in the hyperplane. The tables are based on the assumption that the same number of variables are in the hyperplane of each of the factors being compared.[30] Since this index makes sense, is so easy to calculate with paper and pencil, and has an approximate test of significance, I suggest it strongly as one of (hopefully) several measures used. I should emphasize that one should not blindly calculate all possible S coefficients for all pairs of factors across studies, not indeed any other associational measure, since the likelihood of capitalizing on chance results increases radically (Gorsuch, 1974: 254).

As indicated earlier, an alternative to comparing the factors across studies with all study-specific idiosyncracies left in, is to rotate the two studies to convergence first. In discussing this approach, Rummel (1970) suggests the utilization of the Ahmavaara method by arbitrarily categorizing one or the other of the two studies as the target and rotating the other study to maximum congruence with the pseudo-target. This general suggestion could also be followed using an orthogonal Procrustes program. There have also been several models developed for the joint rotation of both matrices into some common space in which they are maximally congruent. The reader is directed to the articles of Cliff (1966) and Taylor (1967) for discussions of these somewhat more complicated techniques for which there seem to be no widely distributed programs. For most purposes, the utilization of the target analysis programs should sufficiently remove the differences due to study-specific effects.

I must admit some personal bias against joint rotation or using target rotation to line up two empirical matrices for the purpose of evaluating whether the "same" set of factors has been uncovered. My position is captured in large part by the Cattell/Baggeley caveat quoted earlier on the naming of the Procrustes routine. Since we know very little about how well to expect two matrices to fit when they are unrelated and we have no established tests of significance to help inform our judgments, I feel very hesitant to apply these techniques. Perhaps the most convincing argument against these methods comes from a Monte Carlo study done by Nesselroade and Baltes (1970). They generate sets of random numbers, factor analyze these sets individually, and then rotate pairs of these factor matrices to convergence using a modification of Taylor's approach. After the rotation of each pair of matrices, the coefficient of congruence, CC, is calculated between the pair of first factors, the pair of second factors, ... up to the fifth factors. They find that it is not unusual to get CC's in the

.7 to .9 range, indeed some above .9, based on the comparison of rotated matrices generated from random numbers.

Admittedly they find that the average level of the CC's varies with the total number of factors extracted, number of variables, number of cases, and serial number of the pair of factors being compared. Nevertheless, if one can adjust random number factor results so that they converge with CC's typically above .5, then one wonders if it is not far too easy to establish convergence. At a minimum, I would strongly suggest consulting the authors' tabulated results for threshold values of CC which must be greatly exceeded if one wants to claim convergence in one's empirical, non-random data sets. Since these authors provide results for a limited number of combinations of numbers of variables, cases, and factors, one may have to extrapolate from their table or, perhaps better, generate random number matrices equal to the dimensions of one's substantive data and replicate these authors' methods to get a decent baseline level for adequate fit.

As an illustrative problem, I have factor analyzed the variables from the socioeconomic and political set in the canonical correlation example. I divided the cases included in the data set into two groups, those independent prior to 1945 and those which gained independence after 1945. For the purpose of the example I will consider the factor structure of the older nations to be the target configuration and will ask whether the pattern of interdependencies among these six variables is the same in the new nations as in the older group. Table 7 contains the factor loading matrix for the two groups with the results for the new nations labeled F_1 and for the older nations F. The factoring procedures for the two groups were the same, a principal components analysis with a varimax rotation of the first three factors with pairwise deletion of cases with missing data.

At the foot of Table 7, I report a variety of the summary statistics which I have discussed above as possible means to compare factor matrices. From visual inspection of the two matrices, I chose to pair the factors in the same order they were extracted, that is, f_1 with f_1, and so forth. I present both factor by factor results and several overall measures of the fit of the matrices. It is quite clear, both visually and statistically, that the economic development cluster defines the first factor in both groups of cases, or if one were considering F as a hypothesized target configuration there would be strong evidence in support of the hypothesis. One might point to the discrepancy in the loading of ELECT, but this seems trivial in comparison to the three dominant loadings. Across all of the vector summary measures, the root mean square (RMS), coefficient of congruence (CC), Pearsonian correlation (r), and the salient variable similarity index (S), one finds an indication of far greater than chance correspondence. The same conclusion characterizes the comparison of the

TABLE 7
Loading Matrices and Comparison Statistics

	F_1 (New nations)			F (Old nations)		
POP	-.06	-.28	.75	.05	.04	.95
DENS	-.04	.84	-.11	.09	.94	.09
LIT	.45	.65	.39	.83	.26	-.05
ENERGY	.98	.00	-.02	.93	.04	.10
GNP/POP	.97	.11	.01	.96	.10	-.03
ELECT	.06	.37	.77	.40	.43	-.32

Comparison statistics

F_1 vs. F	RMS	CC	r	S
f_1	.22	.94	.93	.86
f_2	.21	.90	.83	.89
f_3	.50	.37	.25	.00
overall	.34	.79	.65	

second factors, with LIT's loading not quite on target. Again the visual and statistical conclusions are the same. The third factors, however, do not converge to any acceptable degree. Although the loading of POP is consistent, there is the clear problem of ELECT and, to a lesser degree, LIT. All of the summary measures suggest that these factors do not match. The overall measures comparing these two matrices as given suggest less than a convincing affirmation that they converge.

Given these results, one might choose to rotate the matrix of the newer nations to see if the inconsistencies might be due to unique properties of the analysis. For the purpose of this demonstration, I calculated an Ahmavaara transformation matrix, T_A, which is presented in Table 8. In that table, I also provide the rotated matrix, $F^* = F_1 T_A$, and the error matrix, $E = F - F^*$, as well as the summary statistics. As one would expect, the rotation has improved the fit of the two matrices. The slight discrepancies of the loadings of LIT and ELECT on first factor have been rotated away, producing a nearly perfect fit. The results for the other two factors have improved, marginally in the case of factor 2, more so for factor 3. I would still conclude that there is no significant fit on the last factor since it is quite clear that statistical results of the magnitudes reported for the third factor could have been produced purely by chance. The overall summary statistics indicate the noticeable improvement in the fit of the two matrices produced by the transformation. I leave it to the reader to decide how to interpret a result in which the matrices fit rather well overall, but one factor clearly does not converge.

The final exercise I present is reported in Table 9. In this run, I constructed a dummy variable, labeled OLDNEW, on which all new nations received a score of one, all old nations a zero. I factored the same six variables along with OLDNEW. This run provides no information concerning the similarity of the factor structures, indeed on this run I have made the assumption that the structure is the same in the two groups. Rather, the results, in particular the loadings of OLDNEW, indicate the factors for which the two groups' factor scores will be most different. The substantive interpretation would be that old nations have noticeably higher factor scores on the first factor (economic development), somewhat lower scores on the second (density), and marginally higher on the last (population size). This kind of analysis should be viewed as exploratory since the inclusions of the dummy variable(s) might influence the factor structure. Thus I would suggest calculating factor scores from a run without the dummy variable(s) and then performing a standard analysis of variance.

TABLE 8
Transformation Results and Comparison Statistics

	$F^* \ (F_1 T_A)$			$E \ (F - F^*)$		
POP	.10	-.13	.38	-.05	.17	.57
DENS	.16	.67	-.32	-.07	.27	.41
LIT	.75	.56	-.05	.08	-.30	.00
ENERGY	.95	-.06	.01	-.02	.10	.09
GNP/POP	.98	.04	-.02	-.02	.06	-.01
ELECT	.41	.40	.18	-.01	.03	-.50

T_A

.98	-.05	.02
.28	.82	-.33
.31	.13	.39

Comparison Statistics

F_1^* vs. F

	RMS	CC	r	S
f_1	.05	1.00	.99	.80
f_2	.19	.91	.84	.75
f_3	.35	.52	.50	.00
overall	.23	.89	.83	

TABLE 9
Factor Loadings, Run with Group Membership Variable

POP	-.04	-.11	.91
DENS	.01	.90	-.02
LIT	.84	.19	.16
ENERGY	.89	-.04	-.05
GNP/POP	.94	.01	.00
ELECT	.39	.33	.45
OLDNEW	-.57	.39	-.20

Analyzing Change Data

To this point in this section, I have assumed that the factor structures being compared were based on different sets of cases. I will now consider briefly the situation in which one has data on the same set of cases on two or more occasions. One might be considering some group of subjects before and after some treatment, for example, data on the attributes of nations before and after World War II. I am assuming throughout this discussion that one has nominally the same variables across occasions. Such analyses might be characterized as investigations of change data. My presentation will be brief since anything beyond a synoptic discussion would require considerable elaboration. Some useful places to begin additional readings on the general issues in analyzing change data are Harris (1963) and Coleman (1968).

Let us assume that we have two sets of data, X_1 and X_2, composed of the same variables measured on the same cases at times t_1 and t_2. Several ways of approaching the analyses of these data suggest themselves. If one were interested in the linkages between the earlier and later data, one might use the canonical procedures presented earlier. Alternatively one might be interested in the ways in which the changes in the variables went together. In this case one might form a matrix of differences, $D = X_2 - X_1$, and then factor the matrix D. If one were interested in the hypothesis that the patterns of inter-dependencies among the variables had not changed over time, one might want to factor each matrix separately and test for convergence through a target routine. As noted in an excellent article by Hakstian (1973), there are a broad variety of plausible rival models to consider in comparing the factor structures from several occasions. Essentially, Hakstian alerts us to the fact that quite different estimation procedures are appropriate depending on what aspects of the general factor equation one assumes are free to vary between occasions.

The general factor equation takes the form:

$$X = ZF + E$$

where X is the matrix of manifest variables, that is, observed scores, Z the matrix of factor scores, F the factor pattern matrix, and E the matrix of errors. Consider this model with data drawn from two occasions:

$$X_1 = Z_1 F_1 + E_1$$

$$X_2 = Z_2 F_2 + E_2$$

Hakstian applies a variety of constraints on this general two occasion model and determines the appropriate method for estimating the required matrices. The most severely constrained model is the one in which both the component scores and pattern matrices are assumed to be the same on both occasions. The model then becomes:

$$X_1 = ZF + E_1$$
$$X_2 = ZF + E_2$$

with the criterion function that the sum of squared errors be minimized. This model is estimated by the simple procedure of averaging the data matrices and factoring the over-occasion means.[31] The second model which Hakstian considers allows the component scores to vary but assumes a constant pattern matrix:

$$X_1 = Z_1 F + E_1$$
$$X_2 = Z_2 F + E_2$$

He considers this a reasonable model for longitudinal data in that it allows for maturation and other causes of differential growth rates while still assuming the consistency of interdependencies in the cross-section. It is, however, not the case that a simple trick will allow easy estimation of this model and some rather elaborate calculations are required. Other models are presented which make alternative assumptions and are estimated in different ways. The point of this discussion is that there is no single correct algorithm for the estimation of the similarity between change data factor matrices.

Hakstian's article—along with such other works as Corballis (1973), Corballis and Traub (1970), Evans (1967), and Tucker (1953, 1966)—gives a variety of approaches appropriate once one has fully specified the model in which one is interested. in other words, one cannot simply apply all of the various models for the analysis of change data and see which one fits the data best. Even if one were to allow this kind of brutal approach to model selection, there are no developed measures of goodness of fit to aid in the selection of the "correct" or applicable model. Once one has selected a model—that is, decided whether it is reasonable to assume that the factor scores have not changed, whether the relationship of the observed variable and the factors might have altered, whether changes are assumed to be orthogonal within and between occasions—then one can select the correct procedure from the alternatives in the literature. Since there are so many possibilities, I merely alert the reader to the problem and the location of certain limited solutions.

CONCLUDING REMARKS

I have tried in this paper to provide an introduction to several multivariate data analytic techniques. In addition to increased familiarity with the terminology of these techniques, I hoped that these discussions would permit the researcher to employ them with some feeling of confidence that the output from the computer will be understood. I have rather consciously left out some rather elegant topics and slighted some rather important research, perhaps most critically the work of Ahmavaara (1954a) and Meredith (1964a,b) on factoring under multivariate selection. I feel that there are sufficient complexities in the material that I have covered to confuse someone new to these matters. I leave my bibliography as a source of further reading for the adventuresome. I also remind the reader that I have been at several points in this volume rather more opinionated than is conventional in methodological texts. It is my presumption that the author of a work like this has two basic responsibilities: first, to provide some basic information concerning the methods and options involved in the various techniques and second, to provide guidance on the basis of supposedly informed judgment in the selection among alternatives.

NOTES

1. Since any linear transformation of the variables $\underline{x}$ and $\underline{y}$—for example, a + b$\underline{x}$ and c + d$\underline{y}$, where a,b,c,d are arbitrary constraints—would have exactly the same correlation as $\underline{x}$ and $\underline{y}$, the mathematics of canonical analysis imposes constraints on the mean and standard deviation of the composite scores such that a unique solution is obtained.

2. As I was reminded by Lawrence Mayer, Statistics Department, Virginia Polytechnic Institute and State University, the absence of correlation implies statistical independence if, and only if, the data are normally distributed. A technically correct phrase is "uncorrelated patterns."

3. It turns out that the coefficients can only be identified up to an arbitrary scalar and the choice of a value for this scalar affects the standard deviation of the resultant canonical variates. It does not, however, affect the canonical correlation.

4. The assumption that X and Y are standardized implies that $(A' Rxx A) = (B' Ryy B) = I$, where A', B' are the tranposes of A and B. To produce the required A and B matrices, given A* and B*, one forms two diagonal matrices, C and D, which contain the square roots of the diagonal elements of the matrices $(A*' Rxx A*)$ and $(B*' Ryy B*)$. One then forms the appropriately scaled A and B matrices by the equations:

$$A = A* C^{-1}$$
$$B = B* D^{-1}$$

that is, post-multiplying the original matrix of coefficients by the inverse of these diagonal matrices. If one remembers that the inverse of a diagonal matrix is formed by replacing the diagonal elements their reciprocal, $(a_{ii})^{-1} = (1/a_{ii})$, and the matrix multiplications required to construct C and D are straightforward, the researcher who lacks programming skills should not feel that these calculations are all that difficult to do by hand.

5. Meredith (1964c: 55-56), supporting the utilization of the structure matrix, suggests "correcting" the correlations for the effects of error in measurement, that is, the unreliability of the data. Calculating the reliability of the canonical variates is a rather simple matter if one treats the variate as a scale composed of weighted items.

6. I do not know of any literature on tests of significance of the individual regression coefficients, that is, the a's and b's, but I have been advised in a personal communication from Professor Mayer that it is appropriate to test the elements of the structure matrix for significance by Fisher's arctangent transformation. Mayer indicates that this test is approximate but asymptotically correct.

7. These tests are based on certain properties of the determinants of matrices as developed by Wilks and are discussed in conventional multivariate statistics texts, such as Anderson (1958: ch. 9).

8. See Anderson (1958: 166-173) for an extensive presentation of the generalized variance, defined there as the determinant of the covariance matrix.

9. There are other related measures in the literature based on functions of the product, V,

$$V = \prod_{i=1}^{k} (1 - r_{ci}^2),$$

specifically Rozeboom's (1965) development of the between-set correlation coefficient, $R_{X,Y}$,

$$R_{X,Y} = (1 - V)^{1/2}$$

I reject such measures, as does Hooper, since V goes to zero if there is a single perfect link, that is, one element of Rxy equalling unity. Thus, such measures do not behave well.

10. Cooley and Lohnes mention the simultaneous independent development of this method of analysis by Miller (1969). What purports to be a scathing critique of the Stewart-Love approach has been published by Nicewander and Wood (1974). Since the critique seems based on some rather outlandish misreadings of the original paper and inadequate demonstrations or proofs of some important points, I will basically ignore the points raised by the critics. It is the case that Stewart and Love are also guilty of claiming things to be true without explicit proof but Cooley and Lohnes' presentation helps solidify the procedure.

11. Stewart and Love (1968: 161) assert *without proof* that the sum of the redundancy coefficients for a set is the mean squared multiple correlation of each of the set's variables regressed on the variables in the other set. This would be another useful interpretive angle but, without proof from the authors, I cannot attest to their claim. Nicewander and Wood (1974: 93) say that the coefficient "clearly" cannot be the mean squared multiple correlation, but neither is their case clear.

12. The data were provided as an SPSS system file from the Inter-University Consortium for Political Research.

13. With the exceptions of the F test and the trace coefficient, the remainder of these statistics were produced by SPSS.

14. For the purpose of this paper, I will act as if it is meaningful to talk of statistical significance in such political science-typical exercises as this one. My apologies to purists.

15. Although I performed the calculation of the structure matrix through the matrix manipulative capabilities of OMNITAB, I could have equally easily used SPSS COMPUTE cards and a call to PEARSON CORR:

		weight		variable	mean	standard deviation
COMPUTE	X =	−.24	*	((POP	− 22808.3)	/ 42195.3)
		−.04	*	((DENS	− 79.4)	/ 89.5) − . . . .
COMPUTE	Y3 =	1.0	*	((DEF	− 3.3)	/ 2.6)
		−.54	*	((EDUC	− 3.7)	/ 1.6)
PEARSON CORR		POP, DENS, LIT, ENERGY, GNPPOP, ELECT				
		WITH X1 to X3/DEF, EDUC, HEALTH				
		WITH Y1 to Y3				

As with any use of computed variables in the presence of missing data, one should in some way, for example, through the use of SELECT IF cards, insure that the canonical variates are calculated only for the cases whose data generated the weights.

16. I should note here that if, as perhaps an econometrically oriented analysis might do, one were using canonical analysis to estimate parameters of a multi-equation system, as suggested by Hooper (1959), then the regression coefficient matrix would be the matrix of interest. I am assuming that political science consumers of canonical analysis would likely not use this technique for that purpose.

17. Having done the preliminary factoring of the original data, one can work backward toward some knowledge of the correlations of the original variables with the ultimate canonical variates. Since the structure and regression coefficient matrices are the same in the orthogonal case, the standard output from the canonical routine will provide the correlation of the intermediate factors with the canonical variates. From the preliminary factor analysis, one should have the correlations of the original variables with the resultant factors. The correlation of the original variable with the final canonical can be calculated by the multiplication of the variables loading on the factor times the factor's correlation with the variate. Unfortunately there is no assurance that the canonical variates defined by canonically correlating factor scores will have similar content to those defined by operating on the original data. This method is clearly not a method of choice.

18. I find it instructive that the term "missing data" does not appear in the indices of the four multivariate texts that I have mentioned: Anderson (1958), Cooley and Lohnes (1971), Tatsuoka (1971), and Van de Geer (1971). Rummel (1970: 258-267) provides a useful discussion of the issue in the context of factor analysis.

19. Obviously I am ignoring the differences in signs across equations since these are artifacts of the orientation of the eigenvector. The content of the variates in an equation would not be changed by multiplying both sets of coefficients by −1.0.

20. In matrix notation, the Darlington method is to calculate $R^* = DRD$, where D is a diagonal matrix of the reciprocals of the square roots of the reliabilities, while the Van de Geer technique is $R^* = R − E$, where E is a diagonal matrix of estimates of the error variance, that is, one minus the square of the reliability.

21. This would take the form of computing $X.Z = X - BZ$ and $Y.Z = Y - CZ$, where B and C are matrices of regression coefficients and X.Z and Y.Z are matrices of residuals. Then the matrices of residuals are submitted to the canonical routine. Alternatively I would find it simpler to calculate the partial bivariate correlations and input the matrix R.Z into the canonical routine. Although the principal diagonal would still contain unities in both computational approaches, it is not clear that the significance tests would continue to be interpretable as in the conventional method.

22. This assumes that one has administered equivalent batteries of stimuli in the two nations such that it is meaningful to assert that the variables are substantively comparable across locations.

23. Perhaps one additional reason for the choice of canonical over target analysis is the relatively broad availability of packaged canonical routines as opposed to the scarcity of factor comparison routines in the widely distributed macropackages. Although there are two factor comparison routines in OSIRIS, for performing Ahmavaara or Schonemann/Carroll analyses, to be discussed below, users without access to OSIRIS will either have to import a stand-alone program or do some moderately complex coding. For those with programming skills, however, most of the authors of methods discussed in this section have been quite helpful in providing in their articles a suggested flowchart or computational steps.

24. Here I will assume that the target matrix could be either specified only by one's theory or could be drawn from previously performed analyses as in the case where one tests whether the multivariate structure of a subsample of cases is the same as the full sample's structure.

25. It is actually the case that the interfactor correlation matrix, R_f, is unchanged. In the case of orthogonal factors, R_f is the identity matrix, I. Whatever R_f is for the factors of F_1, the same matrix will characterize the factors of F^*, that is, R_f is unaffected by the transformation.

26. The discussion in the crucial articles by Meredith (1964a,b) on this point are well worth reading if one has the necessary mathematical skills.

27. On occasion, elements of F^* may exceed unity, especially in the oblique Ahmavaara solution.

28. By the same pattern I mean that the two sets are proportional, $f_{1i} = cf_{2i}$. This suggests that the Pearsonian correlation may be suboptimal as a test since it is based on fit to a function with a non-zero intercept, that is, $f_{1i} = bf_{2i} + d$, $d \neq 0$. As an alternative, one would expect that the ratios of the loadings, f_{1i}/f_{2i}, should all be equal to the same constant c. The standard deviation of these ratios should be very small and might provide a useful comparative test. Obviously the existence of near-zero loadings in f_2 would provide some difficulties in the calculations.

29. Cattell conceptualizes factors as the causes of variance in observable variables.

30. The authors indicate that if this assumption is not viable in one's results, then the average count could be used to enter the tables, although the exact distribution could not be expected to hold.

31. It develops that this model extends to the n-occasion case by taking averages across all occasions.

REFERENCES

AHMAVAARA, Y. (1954a) "The mathematical theory of factorial invariance under selection." Psychometrika 19 (March): 27-38.

——— (1954b) "Transformation analysis of factorial data." Annales Academiae Scientiarum Fennicae 88: 1-150.

ANDERSON, T. W. (1958) An Introduction to Multivariate Statistical Analysis. New York: Wiley.

ARMSTRONG, J. S. and P. SOELBERG (1968) "On the interpretation of factor analysis." Psychological Bul. 70: 361-364.

BARTLETT, M. S. (1948) "Internal and external factor analysis." British J. of Psychology, Statistical Sect. 1: 73-81.

——— (1941) "The statistical significance of canonical correlations." Biometrika 32: 29-38.

BLOXOM, B. (1968) "Factorial rotation to simple structure and maximum similarity." Psychometrika 33 (June): 237-247.

BROWNE, M. and W. KRISTOF (1969) "On the oblique rotation of a factor matrix to a specified pattern." Psychometrika 34 (June): 237-248.

CATTELL, R. B. (1965) "The configurative method for surer identification of personality dimensions, notably in child study." Psychological Reports 16: 269-270.

——— (1962) "The basis of recognition and interpretation of factors." Educational and Psychological Measurement 22: 667-697.

——— (1944) "Parallel proportional profiles and other principles for the choice of factors by rotation." Psychometrika 9: 267.

——— and A. R. BAGGALEY (1960) "The salient variable similarity index for factor matching." British J. of Statistical Psychology 13 (May): 33-46.

CATTELL, R. B., K. R. BALCAR, J. L. HORN, and J. R. NESSELROADE (1969) "Factor matching procedures: an improvement of the s index; with tables." Educational and Psychological Measurement 29: 781-792.

CLIFF, N. (1966) "Orthogonal rotation to congruence." Psychometrika 31: 33-42.

COLEMAN, J. S. (1968) "The matematical study of change," in H. M. Blalock and A. B. Blalock (eds.) Methodology in Social Research. New York: McGraw-Hill.

COOLEY, W. W. and P. R. LOHNES (1971) Multivariate Data Analysis. New York: Wiley.

CORBALLIS, M. C. (1973) "A factor model for analysing change." British J. of Mathematical and Statistical Psychology 26: 90-97.

——— and R. E. TRAUB (1970) "Longitudinal factor analysis." Psychometrika 35 (March): 79-98.

DARLINGTON, R. B. (1968) "Multiple regression in psychological research and practice." Psychological Bul. 69: 161-182.

———, S. L WEINBERG, and H. J. WALBERG (1973) "Canonical variate analysis and related techniques." Rev. of Educational Research 43 (Fall): 433-454.

DIXON, W. J. [ed.] (1970) BMD: Biomedical Computer Programs. Berkeley: Univ. of California Press.

ECKART, C. and G. YOUNG (1936) "The approximation of one matrix by another of lower rank." Psychometrika 1: 211-218.

EVANS, G. T. (1967) "Factor analytical treatment of growth data." Multivariate Behavioral Research 2 (January): 109-134.

GORSUCH, R. L. (1974) Factor Analysis. Philadelphia: Saunders.

GREEN, B. F. (1952) "The orthogonal approximation of an oblique structure in factor analysis." Psychometrika 17: 429-440.

HAKSTIAN, A. R. (1973) "Procedures for the factor analytic treatment of measures obtained on different occasions." British J. of Mathematical and Statistical Psychology 26: 219-239.

HALL, C. E. (1969) "Rotation of canonical variates in multivariate analysis of variance." J. of Experimental Education 38: 31-38.

HANNAN, E. J. (1967) "Canonical correlation and multiple equation systems in economics." Econometrica 35 (January): 123-138.

HARMAN, H. H. (1967) Modern Factor Analysis. Chicago: Univ. of Chicago Press.

HARRIS, C. W. [ed.] (1963) Problems in Measuring Change. Madison: Univ. of Wisconsin Press.

HOGBEN, D., S. T. PEAVY, and R. N. VARNER (1971) OMNITAB II: User's Reference Manual. Washington, D.C.: Natl. Bureau of Standards.

HOOPER, J. W. (1962) "Partial trace correlations." Econometrica 30 (April): 324-331.

——— (1959) "Simultaneous equations and canonical correlation theory." Econometrica 27: 245-256.

HORST, P. (1961a) "Generalized canonical correlations and their applications to experimental data." J. of Clinical Psychology 18: 331-347.

——— (1961b) "Relations among $\underline{m}$ sets of measures." Psychometrika 26 (June): 129-149.

HOTELLING, H. (1936) "Relations between two sets of variables." Biometrika 28: 321-377.

——— (1935) "The most predictable criterion." J. of Educational Psychology 26: 139-142.

HURLEY, J. R. and R. B. CATTELL (1962) "The Procrustes program: producing direct rotation to test a hypothesized factor structure." Behavioral Science 7: 258-262.

JÖRESKOG, K. G. (1969) "A general approach to confirmatory maximum likelihood factor analysis." Psychometrika 34: 183.

——— (1966) "Testing a simple structure hypothesis in factor analysis." Psychometrika 31: 165-178.

——— and D. N. LAWLEY (1968) "New methods in maximum likelihood factor analysis." British J. of Mathematical and Statistical Psychology 21: 85.

KERLINGER, F. K. (1973) Foundations of Behavioral Research, sec. ed. New York: Holt, Rinehart & Winston.

LEEGE, D. C. and W. L. FRANCIS (1974) Political Research: Design, Measurement and Analysis. New York: Basic Books.

McKEON, J. J. (1966) "Canonical analysis: some relations between canonical correlation, factor analysis, discriminant function analysis, and scaling theory." Psychometric Monographs 13: 1-43.

MEREDITH, W. (1964a) "Notes on factorial invariance." Psychometrika 29 (June): 177-185.

——— (1964b) "Rotation to achieve factorial invariance." Psychometrika 29 (June): 187-206.

——— (1964c) "Canonical correlations with fallible data." Psychometrika 29 (March): 55-65.

MILLER, J. K. (1969) "The development and application of bi-variate correlation: a measure of statistical association between multivariate measurement sets." SUNY-Buffalo: Ed.D. dis.

MORRISON, D. F. (1967) Multivariate Statistical Methods. New York: McGraw-Hill.

NESSELROADE, J. R. and P. B. BALTES (1970) "On a dilemma of comparative factor analysis: a study of factor matching based on random data." Educational and Psychological Measurement 30: 935-948.

NICEWANDER, W. A. and D. A. WOOD (1974) "Comments on 'A generalized canonical correlation index.'" Psychological Bul. 81 (January): 92-94.

NIE, N. H., D. H. BENT, and C. H. HULL (1970) SPSS: Statistical Package for the Social Sciences. New York: McGraw-Hill.

OVERALL, J. E. (1974) "Marker variable factor analysis: a regional principal axes solution." Multivariate Behavioral Science 9 (April): 149-164.

PHILLIPS, W. R. (n.d.) "Introduction to canonical analysis." Ohio State Univ.: mimeo.

PINNEAU, S. R. and A. NEWHOUSE (1964) "Measures of invariance and comparability in factor analysis for fixed variables." Psychometrika 29 (September): 271-281.

PLEASE, N. W. (1973) "Comparison of factor loadings in different populations." British J. of Mathematical and Statistical Psychology 26: 61-89.

PRZEWORSKI, A. and H. TEUNE (1970) The Logic of Comparative Social Inquiry. New York: Wiley.

ROZEBOOM, W. W. (1965) "Linear correlations between sets of variables." Psychometrika 30 (March): 57-71.

RUMMEL, R. J. (1970) Applied Factor Analysis. Evanston: Northwestern Univ. Press.

RUSSETT, B. M. (1967) International Regions and the International System. Chicago: Rand McNally.

RUTHERFORD, B. M. (n.d.) "Canonical correlation in political analysis." Northwestern Univ.: mimeo.

RYDER, R. G. (1967) "Computational remarks on a measure for comparing factors." Educational and Psychological Measurement 27: 301-304.

SCHATZOFF, M. (1966) "Exact distribution of Wilk's likelihood ratio criterion." Biometrika 53: 347-358.

SCHONEMANN, P. H. (1966) "A generalized solution of the orthogonal Procrustes problem." Psychometrika 31 (March): 1-10.

——— and R. M. CARROLL (1970) "Fitting one matrix to another under choice of a central dilation and a rigid motion." Psychometrika 35 (June): 245-255.

STEWART, D. and W. LOVE (1968) "A general canonical correlation index." Psychological Bul. 70: 160-163.

TATSUOKA, M. M. (1971) Multivariate Analysis. New York: Wiley.

TAYLOR, C. L. and M. C. HUDSON (1972) World Handbook of Social and Political Indicators, sec. ed. New Haven: Yale Univ. Press.

TAYLOR, P. A. (1967) "The use of factor models in curriculum evaluation: a mathematical model relating two factor structures." Educational and Psychological Measurement 27: 305-321.

THEIL, H. (1971) Principles of Econometrics. New York: Wiley

TUCKER, L. R. (1966) "Some mathematical notes on three-mode factor analysis." Psychometrika 31 (September): 279-311.

TUCKER, L. R. (1958) "An inter-battery method of factor analysis." Psychometrika 23 (June): 11-136.

VAN DE GEER, J. P. (1971) Introduction to Multivariate Analysis for the Social Sciences. San Francisco: Freeman.

VELDMAN, D. J. (1967) Fortran Programming for the Behavioral Sciences. New York: Holt, Rinehart & Winston.

WRIGLEY, C. and J. NEUHAUS (1955) "The matching of two sets of factors." American Psychologist 10: 418-419.

MARK S. LEVINE is an analyst in the Research Department of Leo Burnett, U.S.A., a Chicago-based advertising agency. He has previously served on the faculties of Northwestern University and Southern Illinois University–Carbondale. He received his Ph.D. in political science from the University of Pennsylvania.

Quantitative Applications in the Social Sciences

(a Sage University Papers Series)

$6.50 each

SAGE PUBLICATIONS, INC.
P.O. BOX 5084
NEWBURY PARK, CALIFORNIA 91359—9924

Place
Stamp
here